Wilfred Rhodes.

The
IMMORTALS
of English Cricket

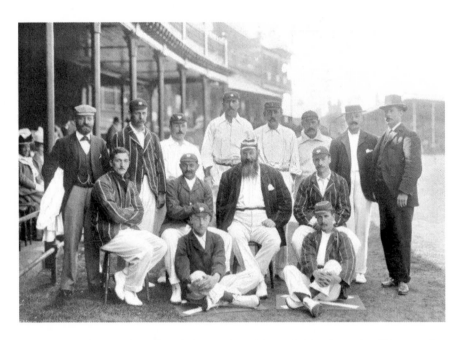

The England team that played Australia at Trent Bridge in 1899. The captain, W G Grace, is unmistakeable in the front row, seated next to the Indian prince, K S Ranjitsinjhi. Wilfred Rhodes is at the front, on the left. This was Rhodes' first Test, and Grace's last.

The
IMMORTALS
of English Cricket

Bill Ricquier

A Gelding Street Press book

An Imprint of Rockpool Publishing, Pty Ltd.

PO Box 252, Summer Hill, NSW 2130

www.geldingstreetpress.com

Published in 2021, by Rockpool Publishing

ISBN 978-1-925946-12-3

Edited by Christopher Cyrill

Images supplied by The Roger Mann Picture Library,
Newspix and Fairfax Media

Printed and bound in China

10 9 8 7 6 5 4 3 2 1

To Anita and Guy with love, and in memory of my late brother Neil, who instilled in me the love of our great game.

CONTENTS

1	Introduction	1
2	Jack Hobbs	11
3	Len Hutton	27
4	Walter Hammond	41
5	Denis Compton	55
6	Ben Stokes	73
7	Ian Botham	87
8	Alan Knott	107
9	Wilfred Rhodes	123
10	Fred Trueman	137
11	Sydney Barnes	155
12	James Anderson	171
13	Afterword	189
14	Acknowledgements	191
15	Bibliography	195
16	About the author	199

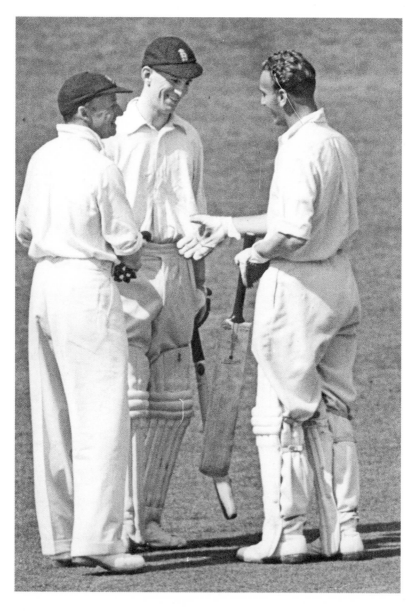

Don Bradman and Joe Hardstaff congratulate Len Hutton on becoming the maker of the highest individual score in Test cricket: England v Australia, The Oval, 1938.

INTRODUCTION

Where do you start?

In his splendid *One Hundred Greatest Cricketers,* published by *The Times* in 1998, John Woodcock, the "sage of Longparish," and, in my opinion, the most influential English cricket correspondent of the last 70 years, chose John Small and "Silver" Billy Beldham, two of the great men from the heyday of the Hambledon club that flourished in the late eighteenth century, and Alfred Mynn, the "Champion, the Lion of Kent," who played in the first half of the nineteenth century; in his list of the top hundred, Woodcock ranks Mynn fourth, between Gary Sobers and Jack Hobbs.

I think that's a bit too early.

No prizes though, for guessing who comes number one in Woodcock's list. Nobody who has been to Lord's and approached the ground from St. John's Wood Road can fail to have been impressed by the ceremonial wrought-iron gates, with the simple and unarguable words above them commemorating the man in whose memory the gates were erected: "The Great Cricketer." W. G. Grace does indeed stand alone in cricket's pantheon. He effectively invented modern batting. But it is the problem of comparing Grace with more "modern" cricketers – it is hard enough to compare him with his contemporaries – that dissuaded me from selecting him.

I might be accused of inconsistency here in that I have selected Wilfred Rhodes, who played with and against Grace; Grace's last match for England was Rhodes' first. But Rhodes was of a different generation. He played on until the 1930s and lived, like S. F. Barnes, until the 1970s.

Wilfred Rhodes, around the time of his surprise recall to the England side for the decisive Test of the 1926 Ashes series.

Woodcock picked a lot of players from the early twentieth century. One I was sorely tempted to choose was the brilliant Indian prince K. S. Ranjitsinjhi, a true genius, inventive as well as prolific.

For the 2000 edition of Wisden Cricketers' Almanack, the editor, Matthew Engel, asked a hundred eminent cricket people from around the world to select their Five Cricketers of the Century. (Pausing here, many readers will know of the Almanack, established by John Wisden in 1864. Anyone who writes more or less seriously about the game is hugely indebted to the "cricketer's Bible." One of the annual features is the editor's choice of Five Cricketers of the Year.)

The Five emerging from the count were Don Bradman (100 votes), Sobers (90 – it seems extraordinary that there were 10 judges who didn't rank Sobers in the top Five), Hobbs, the only Englishman (30), Shane Warne, whose international career started in the last decade of the century (27) and Vivian Richards (25).

Details of the entire voting pattern were published; 49 cricketers received at least one vote, of whom 17 were English (28 of the voters were English). Eight of my Immortals were chosen, Alan Knott being, rather surprisingly, the only eligible omission (Godfrey Evans, with five, was the only wicketkeeper to receive any votes). Woodcock's selection included 40 England players, including seven of the top ten; all mine are there except, of course, James Anderson and Ben Stokes.

In 2009 Christopher Martin-Jenkins produced his *Top 100 Cricketers Of All Time*. Martin-Jenkins' list was, generally, less eccentric than Woodcock's, apart from his insistence on referring to English amateurs by their initials (P. B. H. May and E. R. Dexter, as opposed to Fred Trueman and Brian Statham). He selected 34 England players, again including all mine except Stokes and Anderson. He put Grace at number two and Bradman at number one.

Ben Stokes in typically aggressive mode, at the Melbourne Cricket Ground during the 2013 Boxing Day Test.

In 2015 *David Gower's 50 Greatest Cricketers of All Time* was released (dear old Gower, why choose 100 when 50 will do? Incidentally, Gower was chosen by both Woodcock (72) and Martin-Jenkins (70)). Gower selected 13 England players, including Grace (rather mysteriously inserted at number 10, between Malcolm Marshall and Imran Khan). Again all my selections are there except Anderson and Stokes.

My aim, however, was to choose a well-balanced team, one that could feasibly play an imaginary Test match, a team whose individual abilities would complement one another.

It is also important to settle on some criteria. For me, the important thing was sustained achievement at Test level, against the strongest opposition, which, historically, has tended to mean Australia, South Africa and, at various periods, West Indies, and, in more modern times, India, periodically, Pakistan. (Knott and Botham played no Test cricket against South Africa.) By those standards, my 11 almost picked itself.

Even so, I had nagging doubts about some omissions, and two in particular. The first is Herbert Sutcliffe, who opened the batting in seven successive Ashes series, averaging 66.85. Bradman averaged 89, Steve Smith stands at 64; nobody else has managed more than 58. His overall Test match average was 60.73. Notwithstanding this, it is impossible (as numerous bowlers discovered) to get past the selected openers, two legendary knights of the realm: Sir John Berry Hobbs and Sir Leonard Hutton. Even two more recently knighted openers, Sir Alastair Cook, England's greatest run-scorer, and Sir Geoffrey Boycott, England's greatest controversialist, could not manage that.

The other is Harold Larwood. This was difficult. Like Sutcliffe, Larwood appears in all the above lists – he is equal 17th in the Wisden list. His impact on the cricket of his time was little short of sensational because of Bodyline. But, although he played a part in two other Ashes series wins, in 1926 and 1928–29, his international career, through no fault of his own, was relatively limited.

James Anderson is congratulated by teammate Alastair Cook after dismissing Australian opening batsman Justin Langer during the 2007 New Year's Test at the Sydney Cricket Ground.

The non-selection of Larwood (for this book, not for England) was partly an issue of chronology. The original intention had been to include no current players. But Stokes had such an exceptional summer in 2019 that it seemed absurd to exclude him. And if one includes Stokes, how can one omit England's greatest wicket-taker, Anderson? I wasn't going to drop Trueman, so there was no room for Larwood.

It is a shame that there is also no room for anyone from the 2005 Ashes-winning team. Clearly, however, it is not possible to accommodate Andrew Flintoff along with Stokes and Ian Botham. I make no apologies for saying that Botham was the first name on the team sheet. At least the 2010–11 side is represented by Anderson.

In the foreword to his book, Woodcock said he was tempted to select a couple of players just because he loved watching them play: the Barbadian Roy Marshall, who opened the batting for Hampshire for many years and who, coincidentally, is one of my favourite players, was a case in point. On that basis I would be inclined to pick Gower, and maybe Robin Smith, and even Trevor Jesty (but he never played a Test so that is a problem).

But I am very happy with my chosen 11. I think it has something for everyone. There are three Yorkshiremen (what do they say about a strong Yorkshire meaning a strong England?) There are two from the metropolitan counties of Surrey and Middlesex, and another from the home counties. There are two from the West Country, one from Lancashire, one from Durham and one nomad. There are two things that are most unusual in a modern England side: there is only one top-order left-handed batsman and there is only one player who was born outside the United Kingdom (it's the same player). In terms of statistical achievement, impact on historical (cricketing) events, aesthetic appeal, spectator entertainment and character, it is difficult to see how it can be bettered.

Everybody likes making lists. Well, not everybody, but everyone who does really likes it. Everybody reading this will have their own idea of a team to beat mine on an Elysian field comparable to Lord's or the (old) Adelaide Oval, or Galle, or Worcester (if you're facing the right way[1]).

---

[1] Here is an alternative Eleven: H. Sutcliffe, G. Boycott, K. F. Barrington, P. B. H. May, D. I. Gower, A. W. Greig (c), T. G. Evans, H. Larwood, J. A. Snow, A. V. Bedser, D. L. Underwood.

Fred Trueman, 1961.

Jack Hobbs at The Oval, 1926.

2

JACK HOBBS

Birth date	6 December 1882, died 21 December 1963.
Place of birth	Cambridge
Role	Right-handed opening batsman

John Berry Hobbs was born in Cambridge on 16 December 1882, the oldest child of John and Flora Hobbs. He was the first of 12 children. John senior was a slater's labourer. The part of Cambridge the family lived in, at the time young Jack was growing up, was, according to his biographer Leo McKinstry, noted only for "squalor and poverty ... endless grime, and ceaseless work."

By the time Hobbs died, in 1963, he had been – in the Queen's Coronation Honours of 1953 – the first professional cricketer to be knighted. By now a man of comfortable means, he and the family lived in Wimbledon and he had a successful sports goods business in Fleet Street in the heart of London. And this modest, affable man had re-written the record books of the country's most statistically-obsessed sport, with a classical style and a degree of technical mastery in all conditions that have ensured that his title as England's greatest batsman has never been challenged.

Hobbs' upbringing may have been humble in the extreme, but, as so often is the case of outstandingly high achievers, it was not irrelevant to his development as a player. His father was very keen on cricket and would have loved to become a professional. In the 1880s the popularity of the sport was increasing rapidly in the wake of the star quality of sport's first global icon, the remarkable doctor from Downend, Bristol, W. G. Grace. The furthest John Hobbs got was to become the groundsman at Jesus College, but this enabled his talented little boy to play lots of cricket in the city, especially on Parker's Piece, the celebrated ground where forty or so clubs played. There young Jack attracted the attention of Cambridgeshire's finest, the great Surrey and England opener Tom Hayward. Hobbs qualified for Surrey by two years' residence (it really was a different world) and made his debut for the county, alongside Hayward, as a professional in 1905. His first game for the county was against the Gentlemen of England, led by Grace, then aged 58.

It is worth saying something here about the amateur-professional divide that dominated English cricket until the abolition of the distinction in 1962. That was the last year of the annual fixture – between the wars; there were sometimes two or even three, at The Oval and Scarborough as well as Lord's – between Gentlemen (the amateurs) and Players (the professionals). The professionals played cricket for a living. The amateurs played for fun, or at least, not for money, in theory. The social divide was rigid. On many grounds amateurs and professionals had different dressing rooms and the cricketers entered the field from different gates. No professional captained England in the modern era until Len Hutton was appointed in 1952. He was followed by Peter May, Colin Cowdrey and Ted Dexter, all amateurs.

The system was characterised by cant and hypocrisy. Amateurs were not paid for playing cricket; instead jobs were found for them outside the game. And of course there were their expenses. Grace, of course, was an amateur. It is doubtful whether anyone, except perhaps the odd Indian Premier League millionaire, has ever made more money out of the game.

Hobbs made his first appearance for England in the second Test against Australia at the Melbourne Cricket Ground in 1907–08. He was aged 25, surprisingly old, as McKinstry observes, for someone who was to become so outstandingly successful.

In his first innings in a home Test, the first against Australia at Edgbaston in 1909, he was out for a golden duck, lbw to Charlie McCartney, but he made 62 not out in the second innings, putting on 105 with C. B. Fry at more than a run a ball as England romped home by 10 wickets. M. A. Noble's Australians went on to win the series two-one.

Hobbs missed the last two games with an injured finger. After that he was ever-present. He played in eight Ashes series from 1911/12–1930, and missed just four games – all in 1921, because of illness and injury. Only Don Bradman has scored more than his 11 Ashes centuries (though the Bradmaniac Steve Smith has caught up with him).

Away from the international scene, phenomenal interest was generated in the summer of 1925 as Hobbs approached the record number of first-class hundreds scored in a career, 126, by Grace. In the first part of the 20th century it was assumed that Grace's record would last for ever. (As it happens, Grace is now eleventh on the all-time list, behind, among others, three of Hobbs' contemporaries, Patsy Hendren, Phil Mead and Frank Woolley). Again, such is the relative dearth of interest in domestic cricket, apart from the Vitality Blast of T20, that it is difficult to imagine the degree of interest in, as it happened, Hobbs' rather agonising approach to the record. The only comparable cricketing phenomenon has been Sachin Tendulkar's progress to his hundredth international century. He equalled Grace's record in the first innings of Surrey's game against Somerset at Taunton; in the second innings he exceeded it. He was already 43; he was famously to score a hundred first-class centuries after his 40th birthday.

In the following year, 1926, when the England captain, Arthur Carr, went down with tonsilitis during the Old Trafford Test against Australia, Hobbs acted as stand-in captain, a mark of the respect in which he was universally held. It was, however, a one-off. According to Simon Wilde, "Hobbs possessed the stature but not the personality to break the amateur hold on the leadership."

Jack Hobbs, circa 1920.

In his last Ashes series, in 1930, his returns were relatively modest, by his own standards: 301 runs at an average of 33.44. In the second innings of his last match, at his home ground of The Oval, the Australian team lined up as he walked out to bat, and the captain, Bill Woodfull, called for three cheers. It really was the end of an era, and it was time for the passing of the baton. In that same series Bradman scored 974 runs at an average of 139.14. Eighteen years later, at the same ground, Bradman was to receive a similarly memorable send-off.

Bradman was the ultimate run-machine. Hobbs was somehow more pure and more natural. He had an easy and relaxed stance, perfect eyesight and an almost uncanny judgment of line and length. But there was nothing unusual or idiosyncratic about his basic technique.

What was it, then, that set Hobbs apart, aside from the sheer weight of numbers? To get them out of the way, he made 197 first-class centuries: Hendren is next with 170. He made 61,237 first-class runs: Woolley comes next with 58,969. His Test batting average was 56.94. Here comparisons are more difficult. There are 12 batsmen ahead of him in the list, seven of them exclusively from the post-World War Two era. Two of them are players with whom Hobbs played a lot of his cricket, Herbert Sutcliffe and Walter Hammond. The modern players played a wide variety of Test teams. Hobbs played two Tests against West Indies (two innings, one century, one 50); all his other matches were against Australia and South Africa. In the list of top batting averages nobody else in the top 45 had a career which started before the First World War, when batting conditions were undoubtedly more challenging.

That is perhaps the first thing that set him apart: his ability to make runs on all sorts of wickets. Again, this is something that can be difficult for the modern observer to appreciate. People realise that it remains important to win the toss: wickets, in some ways, wear and "worsen" as time goes on. In Asia, batsmen still encounter the occasional "bunsen" where spin bowlers have a real advantage. But drop-in pitches, and the desire of administrators and television executives to ensure that matches last five days, have given the modern 22 yards a certain homogeneity.

It was very different in Hobbs' day (and indeed in the not so distant past: "Deadly" Derek Underwood won many games for Kent and England on uncovered wickets). As Neville Cardus put it, "... on all kinds of pitches, hard and dry, in this country or in Australia, on sticky pitches here and anywhere else, even on the "gluepot" of Melbourne, or the matting of South Africa, against pace, spin, swing and every conceivable device of bowlers, Hobbs reigned supreme." An early example of this was provided on the MCC tour of South Africa in 1909–10, where the series, won three-two by the home side, was dominated by South Africa's googly bowlers. Aubrey Faulkner and Bert Vogler took 69 wickets between them and the matting wickets employed in South Africa provided special challenges for the Englishmen. Hobbs stood alone. He made 539 runs at an average of 67.37. Only one other England batsman managed an average of 30.

A classic example of a Melbourne "gluepot" came in the second Test in 1920–21, which Australia won by an innings and 91 runs. Hobbs made 122 (out of 251 all out). He put on 142 for the third wicket with Hendren (67) but the combination of heavy rain followed by intense heat made the wicket almost impossible. Hobbs batted for three and a half hours and did not give a chance until after he had reached his hundred. England lost the series five-nil but Hobbs made over 500 runs.

Three years later, in 1924–25 Australia won four games but England at last won one, their first victory in Australia since 1911–12. They won the fourth Test at Melbourne by an innings. Jack Fingleton described the wicket as one of the worst ever known in Melbourne, and the opening partnership of 105 between Hobbs and Sutcliffe as probably the most outstanding in Test history.

There was another "sticky dog" at Melbourne in the third match of the very different 1928–29 series, which England won four-one. England started the sixth day needing 331 to win. Rain delayed the start by an hour and the classic ingredients mixed again to produce a spiteful wicket. Balls frequently lifted from a good length to hit the opening batsmen, Hobbs and Sutcliffe, on the upper body. But they ground it out, putting on 105 for the first wicket, before Hobbs was out for 49. England won by three wickets. In the series as a whole Hobbs made 451 runs at an average of just over 50. He was 46 years old.

Hobbs and Sutcliffe were past masters at this sort of thing. In the fifth Test at The Oval in 1926 the pair set up England's first Ashes series win since 1911–12 with a second innings opening partnership of 172, of which Hobbs made exactly 100. Strangely, this was Hobbs' only Test century at The Oval; in fact, only five of his 17 Test hundreds were made in England. Australia had a first innings lead of 22 when the England openers went in for an anxious hour on the second evening. They survived that but then a tropical storm delayed proceedings on the third morning and then, almost as though it were Melbourne rather than Kennington, out came the sun. In the resulting difficult conditions, the batsmen at first concentrated on survival; Hobbs played the off-spinner Arthur Richardson with almost exaggerated respect, facing him for eight successive overs and scoring two runs. But he flourished at the other end as Australia's captain Herbie Collins became increasingly concerned about how best to exploit the conditions. Hobbs began playing with increasing freedom, sweeping Richardson and hitting Arthur Mailey out of the attack. When he was bowled by Jack Gregory he had batted chancelessly for three and a half hours. The platform was laid for a famous victory.

Hobbs heading out to bat with his usual Surrey opening partner Andrew Sandham, 1930.

Obviously not all Hobbs' great achievements came when conditions were difficult. It cannot be a coincidence that six of the top ten run scorers in first-class cricket, and Bradman, played a significant part of their cricket in the 1920s and/or 1930s. Even so, Hobbs seemed like a man apart. And this is the case despite the fact that in a sense he was two different players.

Three of the other batsmen profiled in this book – Hammond, Hutton and Denis Compton – had their careers interrupted by the global conflict of 1939-45. Hutton and Compton were young enough when the war started for it not really to make a difference to them as players; they were simply older, more mature, and better, when play resumed. For Hammond the issue was, does it make sense to start all over again at 41? Who knows, maybe he got that one wrong.

With Hobbs, it was different. At 37 in 1919, when county cricket resumed after the four-year break caused by the First World War, he was a veteran, but certainly not over the hill, as indeed events proved. He himself, however, admitted that he wasn't the same player after the War. "I was still good," he would say, half in jest, "but I made almost all my runs off the back foot." If anything he was more prolific in the second part of his career. But as the former England captain A. C. Maclaren wrote in 1926, "In spite of all the hundreds he has made recently, he had more strokes in 1914 than he has now, owing to his wisdom in only attempting now what his years will allow him." Hobbs himself said much the same thing: "[T]here is no doubt, when I was young, I thought I could do it all – and I used to. You see I enjoyed it so much and I was making runs all the time – and that was my living. I never took such risks after the war because I didn't feel I could."

All these comments give an indication of the distinction between the pre-War and post-War Hobbs. Pre-War, it is hardly an overstatement to say that he was the English Victor Trumper. No Australian cricket fan can be oblivious to the significance of this comment. "Trumperesque," according to Cardus, "…quick to the attack on springing feet, strokes all over the field, killing but never brutal, all executed at the wrists…"

He was perhaps at the height of his powers on his second tour of Australia, in 1911–12. Maclaren, who had toured with him in 1907–08, said that, "When he came to Australia in 1911–12, though, he was a far more mature, confident – almost assertive – batsman. You could say that he simply did not have a weakness. He was never off balance; and he was so quick without ever having to hurry."

This epic series, an "unprecedented triumph" for England, as McKinstry put it, started very inauspiciously. The captain, Plum Warner, fell ill and was replaced by J. W. H. T. Douglas. Then they lost the first Test, by 146 runs. Ultimately, however, England won the series 4-1. Hobbs was the outstanding batsman on either side, making 662 runs at an average of 82.75, with three centuries. He was, according to Cardus, "Supreme; I doubt if ever after did he surpass for combined offensive and defensive power his batting in this rubber."

McKinstry observed that Hobbs' fielding made a significant contribution to England's victory. With his speed and athleticism he ran out fifteen batsmen during the tour. John Arlott was unambiguous in his praise: by 1914, Hobbs was the greatest cover fielder in the world.

By the time this series started Hobbs had established the first of three celebrated opening partnerships. In his first few Tests he had a number of different partners but in South Africa in 1909–10 he established a batting liaison with the Yorkshireman Wilfred Rhodes that was to last till 1914. At Cape Town in 1909–10 they put on what was then a world record 221. At Melbourne in 1911–12 they added what remains an English Ashes record of 323.

*Hobbs on his way to 115 in the first Test against Australia at Sydney,
1924–25.*

The second famous partnership is that with Andy Sandham, for Surrey. This is outside the scope of this essay in that they never opened together for England but it would be wrong to write about Hobbs without mentioning Sandham. They made no fewer than 66 century opening stands together.

But the opening partner with whom Hobbs will always be associated is another Yorkshireman, Sutcliffe. Sutcliffe averaged a remarkable 60.73 in his 54 Tests. He lacked the style and nobility of Hobbs at the crease; his outstanding features were what Bill Frindall described as, "Determination and unruffled calm."

Hobbs driving in a game versus Warwickshire at The Oval, 1930.

Their record together in Tests, between 1924 and 1930, is phenomenal. They shared 15 three-figure opening partnerships for England. They averaged 87 in Tests as a partnership. Many pairs have been more prolific, because so much more cricket is played, but no other pair have approached this average; Matthew Hayden and Justin Langer managed 51; Gordon Greenidge and Desmond Haynes 47. Among the top 20 run-getting pairs, the second highest average is that of Hobbs and Rhodes (61).

In the second Test of the 1924–25 series in Melbourne they batted throughout the third day, putting on a chanceless 285 (Hobbs, out to the second ball of the fourth day, 154, Sutcliffe, who made four hundreds in the series, 176). As an aside, this was the first time that the future Australian Prime Minister, Robert Menzies, took his wife to watch a Test match. The next time was at Lord's in 1926. The Australian fielders came out and, behind them, emerging from the darkness of the Pavilion, came Hobbs and Sutcliffe. "Goodness," exclaimed Mrs Menzies, "haven't we got these two out yet?"

In the case of both Rhodes and Sutcliffe, there was never any doubt about who the senior partner was. Hobbs is often portrayed as a very unselfish cricketer. Rhodes was one of a number of people who said that Hobbs could have scored many more runs but would often give his wicket away after reaching his hundred. But like it or not top sport inevitably involves an element of selfishness, and batting is perhaps a peculiarly selfish process. Hobbs was a brilliant runner between the wickets – Rhodes said the two of them had a perfect understanding – but Hobbs seems to have had a special penchant for stealing a single off the last ball of the over.

This is one of the little points of criticism made by McKinstry. He also comments, adversely, on Hobbs' use of pad play in defence. This seems a little harsh; under the old lbw law, changed in 1937, a batsman could not be out leg before to a ball which pitched outside the off stump. Hobbs was just exploiting the conditions. (Cardus in fact said Hobbs rarely used his pads as a first line of defence though Wilde, among others, takes a different view.)

More difficult to defend, perhaps, is his conduct in the early part of the First World War. Unlike vast numbers of people, including well-known sportsmen, he declined to enlist, getting a job in a munitions factory which gave him time to get other paid work. More controversially still, in 1916 he signed as a professional in the Bradford League. Lord Hawke, the Yorkshire cricket supremo, called the signing "scandalous." Hobbs joined the Royal Flying Corps. Earlier biographers, such as Arlott, had glossed over this period.

At the end of the day this is a minor issue. McKinstry's verdict is essentially no different from Arlott's. How could it be otherwise. Arlott summed up his idol perfectly: "Others scored faster, hit the balls harder, more obviously murdered bowling. No one else, though, ever batted with more consummate skill." Hence, the name by which he will always be remembered: The Master.

Jack Hobbs

TESTS

Batting & Fielding

M	I	NO	Runs	HS	Ave	100	50	Ct
61	102	7	5410	211	56.94	15	28	17

Bowling

Balls	R	W	Ave	BBI	SR	Econ	
376	165	1	165	1-19	376		

FIRST-CLASS

Batting & Fielding

M	I	NO	Runs	HS	Ave	100	50	Ct
826	1315	106	61237	316*	50.65	197	270	334

Bowling

Balls	R	W	Ave	BBI	5	10	Rate	
5199	2676	107	25	7-56	3	0	48.58	

Two debutants opening the batting for England against New Zealand in the first Test of the 1937 series, at Lord's, a worried looking Len Hutton, and Jim (J H) Parks.

3

LEN HUTTON

Birth date	3 June 1916, died 6 September 1990
Place of birth	Fulneck, Pudsey, Yorkshire
Role	Right-handed opening batsman

Sometimes it's the apparently random, isolated incidents, seemingly small things, that tell you most.

Four such things in the life of Len Hutton.

The first is an innings, played in the second innings of the second Test against Australia at Sydney in 1946–47. England had been annihilated in the first Test at Brisbane by an innings and 332 runs. Now, in Sydney, Australia had made 659 for eight in response to England's 255. Openers Hutton and Cyril Washbrook went in with 25 minutes to go before lunch on the fifth day.

It is difficult to comprehend Hutton's mindset here. If it had been England's first innings, one has to assume his approach would not have been different. And here there was just half an hour to go before an interval. Of course Test batting, including opening batting, has been transformed in modern times, particularly since the Steve Waugh era in Australia. How should an opener approach such a situation, with a day and two sessions to bat out? Rory Burns would no doubt have clear instructions; even David Warner might be reasonably circumspect.

Hutton was out to the last ball before lunch. As he faced a ball from Keith Miller his bat slipped and hit his wicket; the score was 49 for one, Hutton 37.

Ralph Barker called it a "thrilling display." Wisden's match report described Hutton "launching a fierce assault" on the Australian bowlers. Neville Cardus said it was "so dazzling in clean diamond-cut strokes that old men present babbled of Victor Trumper." There can be no higher compliment than that. According to the Yorkshire scribe J. M. Kilburn, who must have watched him bat more than anyone, Hutton on that day "enraptured all Sydney. In his brief glory he laid everyone beneath a spell, carried them on wings of enchantment high above figures, facts, victories and defeats, into the cloudland of imperishable memory." (England lost by an innings and 33 runs.)

Next, 1948. Once again England are two-nil down after two Tests against Australia. The next is due to take place at Old Trafford. Jack Fingleton prepares his readers, "One morning, in the county of Yorkshire, a dour Yorkshireman sat down to breakfast, opened his newspaper, blinked his eyes and said, 'Wife, don't speak to me. They've dropped Hutton.'" It was not really clear why Hutton had been dropped. His replacement, George Emmett, was hardly a long-term prospect, playing only the one test. Hutton was back for the fourth.

We are now in 1953, and England were getting steadily better – they actually won the fifth Test in Australia in 1950–51, their first victory over the old enemy since The Oval Test of 1938. Australia weren't getting worse exactly, but their supremacy was being challenged.

And Hutton was captain; England's first full-time professional captain. Initially, he was only appointed for the first three Tests. It had not been that long ago that the Yorkshire autocrat Lord Hawke had said that a professional would captain England over his dead body.

Captain, and the best batsman; Hutton had made a masterly 145 in the second Test at Lord's. The first three Tests were gripping draws. The teams convened at Headingley for the fourth match. Headingley, the home of Yorkshire cricket, and their man was in charge.

Lindsay Hassett won the toss and opted to field.

Hutton was bowled – yorked – second ball for nought by Ray Lindwall. The England captain and outstanding batsman, out second ball in a vital match on his home ground.

Len Hutton batting during his century against Australia in the first Test of the 1938 series at Trent Bridge. Ben Barnett is behind the stumps.

Fingleton again: "Over went his off stump and this huge Yorkshire crowd sat in stunned and pained silence as their idol walked off. There is no silence to compare with that of a crowd which sees its favourite fall."

Finally, Australia 1954–55. Now he was not just captain; he was an Ashes-winning captain. England won The Oval Test in 1953 to take the series one-nil.

Being captain overseas was in some ways more stressful than being captain at home (although in his memoirs Hutton claimed the reverse was the case, from a purely cricketing perspective, because of the vagaries of the English weather). There was, first, what one might call the diplomatic stuff. There were lots of functions at which he had to speak; that was not an issue, Hutton was a polished and amusing speaker. But he did not enjoy the limelight. An underlying issue was the fact of his status as England's first professional captain. Some cricket people, notably the Daily Telegraph correspondent E. W. Swanton (said to be such a terrible snob that he refused to sit in the same car as his own chauffeur) found the notion of a professional as captain hard to take. At this time "England" tours were still organised by the Marylebone Cricket Club. Hutton was officially MCC captain. But he wasn't a member of the Club, and he was uncomfortable about this.

There were also lots of personnel issues: inevitably there were some players on tour he did not really believe in. In England's second innings in the second Test, in Sydney, the graceful Gloucestershire batsman Tom Graveney, was out to a loose shot, playing, according to John Woodcock, "...as though he were well set in a September festival in Weston-super-Mare."

Stephen Chalke, in his book about Geoffrey Howard, who was the manager of the 1954–55 tour, continues the story: "It was a shot that confirmed all his captain's prejudices, as Geoffrey Howard knew well". "I think Len would always have been looking for aspects of Tom's character to uphold his view that he wasn't reliable. He's got a red face, he told me one day, I don't like red faces."

The series could not have got off to a worse start, Australia winning the first Test at Brisbane by an innings and 154 runs after Hutton had won the toss and elected to field.

How could England fight back? Hutton was convinced it had to be through outright pace bowling, while maintaining a balanced attack. Where was the axe to fall?

England's first professional captain meets the new monarch during the Test against India at Lord's, 1952.

The choice was the fast-medium bowler Alec Bedser, who had contracted shingles at the start of the tour and who took one for 131 at Brisbane (compared to new fast man Frank Tyson's one for 160). Bedser had been England's best bowler in the post-war years and remains, arguably, one of her greatest ever; Don Bradman certainly thought so.

Howard, the tour manager, offered to break the news to Bedser but Hutton insisted that it was his job. In Chalke's book, Howard said he should have insisted. He said he would always remember going into the dressing room on the first morning of the second Test at Sydney. The team list had been pinned to the back of the dressing room door. Bedser was standing there in his whites looking at the list to see who was playing. In his own memoirs Hutton said that dropping Bedser was the hardest decision he ever made in cricket, but he rather glossed over the process, although he did say that he spoke to Bedser before the game and explained that he might not be playing.

What do these four things tell us about Hutton? Well, they tell us that he was a very great batsman indeed. That innings in Sydney, that brief spell, just 20 minutes, tells us that. Anyone looking at Wisden and the statistics can see that Hutton was a great player. But that innings tells us something more, that he was a batsman of the purest classical style, comparable to the young Jack Hobbs. The remarkable thing was that it was so unexpected, in the context of the match. Kilburn bumped into Hutton in the lunch interval and commiserated with him. "It's a pity," Hutton replied, "We might have seen something."

It was Hutton's fourth innings of the series. His last innings against Australia before that had been in August 1938, at The Oval, in the England victory mentioned above. That hadn't been a little thing; it was one of cricket's biggest things. Hutton made 364, the highest Test score ever, until overtaken by Gary Sobers in 1957–58. It remains the fourth longest of all Test innings (797 minutes, more than 13 hours). He was 22 years old.

Which was more of an aberration, the 1938 grinding marathon or the 1946–47 spirited frolic? Usually Hutton didn't have much choice as to how he played. As Kilburn put it, "Hutton realised as well as anybody and better than most that fast bowling of the quality presented by Lindwall and Miller cannot be hustled into subjection except on rare occasions. Anything more than temporary domination had to be built on patient resistance and Hutton's task for years was to undertake this responsibility." In four Ashes series between 1946 and 1953, Hutton averaged over 57, but he was on the losing side in 11 games and on the winning side only twice.

It was not as if he was on his own. The inimitable Denis Compton was in his prime, as was his Middlesex "twin", the pugnacious Bill Edrich. Washbrook was a redoubtable opening partner; the two of them put on 359 against South Africa at Johannesburg in 1948–49, still England's record opening partnership. But the pressures and the expectations were always on Hutton.

In the 1950–51 series in Australia, which Australia won four-one, England's batsmen were confronted not only by Lindwall and Miller, but also by mystery spinner Jack Iverson, who took 21 wickets at an average of 15. Hutton made 533 runs at an average of 88.

There was an extraordinary start to the series in Brisbane, when tropical rain made the uncovered pitch a minefield. Having bowled Australia out for 228, England declared on 68 for seven; Australia then declared on 32 for seven. In England's second innings Hutton was held back to number eight: he went in at 30 for six. He played a classically untroubled innings of 62 not out, but he couldn't bat at both ends. England lost by 70 runs.

In the fourth Test at the Adelaide Oval he carried his bat for 156 out of a total of 272. The next highest scorer was captain Freddie Brown with 16. In the series as a whole, Compton averaged 7 and Washbrook 17. (Edrich had not been selected.) Hutton's primacy, the feeling that if he failed, England would fail, explains the shock at his being dropped in 1948, and his abrupt dismissal at Headingley in 1953.

That Adelaide innings was the second time he had carried his bat in six months. The first had been in the fourth and final Test against the West Indies at The Oval in 1950. This time the principal threat came from the two young spinners, Sonny Ramhadin and Alf Valentine. The visitors were two-one up, and, batting first, made 503. England were bowled out for 344 (Valentine four for 131, John Goddard four for 25) and 103 (Valentine six for 39). In that first innings Hutton made 202 not out. Compton was run out for 44, and Reg Simpson made 30; nobody else got 20.

There were a couple of other near misses, in terms of the rare achievement for an opener of carrying his bat. The fifth Test of the 1948 Ashes series, at The Oval, is famous as the occasion of Bradman's last Test innings, bowled for nought. He didn't get a second chance. None was needed. Australia winning by an innings largely because, on the first day, they bowled England out for 52. Hutton was the last man out, for 30, having batted, according to Wisden, "In his customary, stylish, masterful manner."

There was another near miss in the Caribbean in 1953–54, his first tour as captain. The West Indies had won the first two Tests, England the third (Hutton 169), and the fourth had been drawn. So England had to win the fifth, at Sabina Park, to square the series. They did, by nine wickets. Hutton made 205 out of 414 in their first innings, and was seventh out. He batted for almost nine hours in enervating heat and humidity, hitting 24 fours and a six (off Sobers, in his first Test). It was

Hutton's 19th and last Test century, and the first double century made by an England captain overseas.

Stylish. Masterful. These seem like the perfect descriptions of Hutton the batsman. Of average height, and with a comfortable, relaxed stance, he batted in the classical style, driving beautifully in the arc between cover and midwicket. Writing after Sir Leonard's death in 1990, John Woodcock tried to think of modern batsmen who resembled him; he thought Steve Waugh and Mohammed Azharuddin were the closest.

The fourth "incident" – the dropping of Bedser – tells us a lot about Hutton the captain. Hutton is remembered by all English cricket experts as much for his captaincy as his batting. He did something that no one had done before and that only two men: Mike Brearley and Andrew Strauss have done since: he won Ashes series both at home (1953) and away (1954–55). England had previously won the Ashes in 1932–33: 1953 was the 2005 of its time.

Nobody could call him a lucky captain; he lost all five tosses in 1953 (and four of them in the drawn series in the Caribbean in 1953–54). In a sense he wasn't a natural captain – Lord Hawke would have said most unnatural – and he had never captained Yorkshire before he was made England captain in 1952. But he enjoyed the on-field captaincy, and his shrewdness and astute reading of the game made him a sound tactician. And, like all the great captains, he was lucky to have gifted players in his side, especially his leading pace bowlers, Tyson and Brian Statham. Timing really is everything.

And he could be ruthless. It will be recalled that the 1954–55 series got off to a dreadful start at Brisbane. (Years later Sir Leonard was asked by his ghostwriter at The Observer, Scyld Berry, if he knew the Brisbane River: "I thought of throwing myself in there". Berry knew he wasn't joking.)

The ruthlessness wasn't directed at Bedser. Hutton was a kind man and knew Bedser would be hurt. It was directed at the opposition. Hutton did not like facing fast bowling. For much of his cricketing life he had been preoccupied by two of the greatest in Lindwall and Miller. In his memoirs he was to say that he hoped no batsmen in the future would have to face the number of bouncers he and Washbrook had to contend with from the Australian pair. Now it was time for someone else to face the music.

The England side that regained The Ashes at The Oval in 1953. Back row, left to right: T E Bailey, P B H May, T W Graveney, J C Laker, G A R Lock, J H Wardle (12th man), F S Trueman. Front row, left to right: W J Edrich, A V Bedser, L Hutton, D C S Compton, T G Evans.

He had already experienced the pleasure of captaining a side with the sort of raw pace available that could cause real havoc. After two overs of India's second innings in his first Test as captain, at Headingley in

1952, bowled by debutant fast bowler Fred Trueman and Bedser, the scoreboard showed India at nought for four. "Take a good look at it," said Hutton to his team. "You'll never see another like it in a Test."

Trueman didn't go to Australia in 1954–55. There it was Brian Statham and especially Tyson. And it wasn't just the pace. Australian writer Ray Robinson commented on how England's over rate slowed down during the series. At one stage, in Adelaide, Hutton held four mid-over discussions with Statham. As Robinson said, "The fewer overs bowled the greater the proportion of pace turned on and the less respite from high-speed pressure for the batsmen. "Clive Lloyd's West Indians were doing nothing new in the 1980s in this regard. As Woodcock admitted, Hutton was the pioneer.

There is no doubt that the "soft skills" of captaincy eluded Hutton, though he was at pains in his memoirs to assert that he was always trying to encourage his younger players. Up in Yorkshire you didn't mince words. As captain he was perhaps too remote from his younger players; there were issues with Trueman and Tony Lock in the Caribbean in 1953–54 and, as noted above, he never thought the stylish Tom Graveney was reliable. In his memoirs he admits that the Bedser decision caused him great anxiety. But even Woodcock found it hard to excuse the clumsy and heartless way the decision effectively to end a great Test career had been handled.

In fairness to Hutton he was undoubtedly sincere in his assertion about encouraging young players. John Arlott thought he understood Trueman as a bowler, but not as a man. Howard also makes it clear what a tremendous strain the 1954–55 tour was for Hutton. The 1953–54 tour took its toll as well; he missed a month's cricket in 1954 when the amateur David Sheppard took over the captaincy against Pakistan; Swanton's hopes were undoubtedly raised.

The fact was, it was the end of an era. Compton and Edrich were on the tour as well. Hutton and Edrich averaged 24 and 22 respectively, Compton 38. The new stars were the young amateurs, Peter May and Colin Cowdrey. Within a year Hutton had retired, and within two he was a knight of the realm.

It had been a remarkable journey. Born in Pudsey, he made his debut for Yorkshire in 1934 as an 18-year-old. It was a tough old school; Hutton watched, and listened and learned, especially from his opening partner, the great Herbert Sutcliffe. By 1937 he was making a century against New Zealand at Old Trafford in his second Test. He made another in his first Ashes Test, at Trent Bridge, in 1938. Then came The Oval and his 364: he put on 382 for the second wicket with fellow Yorkshireman Maurice Leyland, still an England record.

Then came the war. What might he have achieved but for that? As it happened he injured his left arm in a training accident, and the resulting operation left it two inches shorter than the right.

Photos of Hutton show a face of character and wry humour. In his retirement, in Surrey of all places (for the archetypal Yorkshireman), he was a figure hugely respected throughout the sporting world, occasionally illuminating matters with what Berry termed his "Delphic utterances".

There was a good example at a function soon after the second Test at Sydney in 1954–55. A woman said to him: "Who are the awful people who dropped poor Alec?" "Well, you know," said Hutton, "A good young 'un is always better than a good old 'un."

LEN HUTTON

TESTS

Batting & Fielding

M	I	NO	Runs	HS	Ave	100	50	Ct
79	138	15	6971	364	56.67	19	33	57

Bowling

Balls	R	W	Ave	BBI	SR	Econ	
260	232	3	77.33	1-2	86.66		

FIRST-CLASS

Batting & Fielding

M	I	NO	Runs	HS	Ave	100	50	Ct
513	814	91	40140	364	55.51	129	177	400

Bowling

Balls	R	W	Ave	BBI	5	10	Rate	
9774	5106	173.00	29.51	6-76	4	1	56.49	

Hammond, aged 21, in a Gloucestershire blazer, 1924.

4

WALTER HAMMOND

Birth date	19 June 1903, died 2 July 1965
Place of birth	Dover, Kent
Role	Right-handed middle-order batsman, right-arm medium-fast bowler

Wally Hammond was incapable of performing a graceless act on a cricket field. There is a famous photograph of Hammond, and the Australian wicketkeeper Bert Oldfield, taken during MCC's game against New South Wales, during the 1928–29 tour. It shows Hammond cover-driving, his trademark blue handkerchief protruding from his right hip pocket. The scholarly cricket writer and man of letters, Alan Ross, wrote a poem about this wonderful picture:

"Leonardo would have made him fly,
This batsman is revving with power
He seems airborne."

As is often the case, Jack Fingleton got it just right: "It almost lives, so true is it a description of Hammond's grace, power, correctness and artistry."

Yet, in some ways, Hammond was an unfortunate cricketer.

This may seem a strange thing to say. Of all the players profiled in this book, Hammond was perhaps the most naturally gifted. No less a judge than Neville Cardus called him one of the truly great cricketers in the game's history.

"As a batsman," according to R. C. Roberson-Glasgow, "he had it all, and with double the strength of most players; strength scientifically applied." His stroke-making was both powerful and exquisite. The drive was his great glory, straight and particularly through the covers. "To field to him at cover-point," according to Robertson-Glasgow, "was a sort of ordeal by fire."

Herbert Fishwick's famous photograph of Wally Hammond's cover drive, taken at the Sydney Cricket Ground in 1928. Bert Oldfield is behind the stumps.

Back to Fingleton, and that photograph. And Hammond's signature shot, the cover drive. "If once you have seen Hammond make a cover drive the vision will live with you for all time. See Bradman, McCabe, Kippax, Hobbs, Jackson and the other stylists in a cover drive and there you have the perfect demonstration of that player's skill and style, but none will show you the stroke at its greatest better than Hammond."

As a batsman, his stroke-making was both powerful and exquisite. He made the then highest individual score in Test cricket, 336 against New Zealand in 1932–33, overtaken by Len Hutton's 364 in 1938. He was the first player to exceed 900 runs in a Test series, against Australia in 1928–29. He made 36 double centuries (including four triples) in first-class cricket: only Don Bradman, with 37, made more. Only Bradman, Kumar Sangakkara and Brian Lara scored more than his seven Test scores of 200 or above.

He could have been one of the great all-rounders if he could have been persuaded to bowl more; he took over 700 first-class wickets with an innings best of nine for 23, against Worcestershire.

He was a peerless slip fielder, taking 110 catches in 85 Tests, and 819 in first-class cricket; only three fielders took more. He could, said Robertson-Glasgow, "make with ease a slip catch which others would not merely miss but would not even have rated as a miss."

Something, however, was missing. Despite his pre-eminence as a sportsman, Hammond was commonly regarded as a moody, often solitary figure. He was the subject of endless gossip among teammates – about his mysterious illness, contracted in the West Indies (of which more below) – and about his heritage (some teammates thought he was of Romany descent). When his cricket career was over he took his second wife and their family off to South Africa, where he lived in relative obscurity until his death, aged only 62, in 1965, from the after effects of a car accident that inflicted severe head injuries. John Woodcock, who met Hammond during Mike Smith's tour of South Africa in 1953, thought he was a nicer person after the accident.

Much is revealed in the biography by David Foot, surely the most complete study made of the life of any cricketer. He writes of Hammond's peripatetic and seemingly rather insecure childhood, the loss of his father, a career soldier, in active service during the First World War. He writes of his successful early years with Gloucestershire, and the MCC tour of the West Indies in 1925–26. There, Hammond contracted a mysterious infection, the nature of which was never disclosed: it was assumed to be mosquito borne, like so many bad things emerging from the tropics. Hammond almost died. Foot is as close to being definite as makes no difference in saying that it was syphilis. Hammond, emotionally barely more than a boy at the time, was a changed person once he recovered. Foot attributes Hammond's moodiness – the vast majority of former teammates he interviewed used this as a sort of default description – and bouts of depression, to the toxic brew of medicines he was prescribed in connection with this illness.

Foot also writes about his social ambitions, at a time when, because of the reputations of men like Jack Hobbs and Herbert Sutcliffe, the status of professional cricketers was steadily improving. Hammond was the first professional sportsman to drive a sponsored car. But unlike Hobbs, in particular, being a professional wasn't enough for Hammond. Guided by his mentor, "Plum" Warner, Hammond set about becoming an amateur. Jobs were found for him in Bristol. He achieved his goal in 1937. In the following year he was captaining England against Australia. Even that turned out to be a poisoned chalice, culminating in the unhappy 1946–47 Ashes series.

Wally Hammond, circa 1930.

That tour apart, life on the cricket field was a lot less troubled than off it, as his stellar achievements testify. Business and matrimonial failures cast a shadow, but, once he had established himself there seemed to be no limit to his cricketing achievements. Even then, he must occasionally have felt inclined to rue the timing of his career.

As with so many great England players, Hammond's record is best assessed in the context of Ashes series; he played in seven.

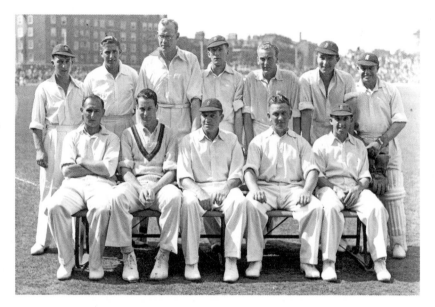

England's team that beat Australia at The Oval in 1938. Back row, left to right: *W J Edrich, C J Barnett (12th man) , W E Bowes, L Hutton, J Hardstaff, D C S Compton, A Wood.* Front row, left to right: *H Verity, K Farnes, W R Hammond, M Leyland, E Paynter.*

In his first, in 1928–29, he made 905 runs in the five Tests; England won the series four-one. He had played eight Tests to date, against South Africa in 1927–28 and West Indies in 1928 but had not yet made an impact internationally. In the first Test at Brisbane, which England won by 675 runs, he made a modest contribution of 44 and 28. In the second Test, at Sydney, he made 251. In the third, at Melbourne, it was 200 and 32. In Adelaide, in the fourth, he scored 119 not out and 177. And finally, back in Melbourne for the fifth Test, which Australia won, he made 38 and 16.

This tour, triumphant as it was, sowed the seeds of the problem that was to confront England throughout the 1930s and beyond. In the match against New South Wales (when the famous photograph was taken) Hammond made a magnificent 225 before being brilliantly run out by a young fielder who proceeded to score an obdurate century and help save the game. His name was Don Bradman.

Bradman was selected for the Brisbane Test but failed and was dropped. Returning for the third Test, he made centuries in both Melbourne Tests.

England, 1930. Australia won the series two-one, sealing their victory with a massive innings win in the fifth Test at The Oval. Hammond had a moderate series, although he scored a hundred in the draw in Headingley. Bradman made 334 there. In all, he made 974 runs in the series. As Ralph Barker put it, "The avalanche of runs from Bradman finally proved suffocating."

Hammond's series record was eclipsed. Another biographer, Ronald Mason observed that, "It is likely that Bradman knew the precise moment when this happened and just as likely that Hammond did not ... As the two greatest batsmen of the thirties, it is as well to see them together at this fleeting moment before the younger soars above his fellow. They were to remain closely conscious of each other for the remainder of their joint careers."

How was Bradman's avalanche to be halted?

England's new captain, the austere, patrician Douglas Jardine, thought he had the answer. The side he led to Australia in 1932–33 was packed with fast bowlers, led by the Nottinghamshire duo, the exceptionally fast Harold Larwood and the left-armer Bill Voce. Bodyline – short-pitched bowling directed at the body, with a posse of close-in leg side fielders, and two more stationed in the deep to deal with a batsman who hooked or pulled – was the method. England won the series four-one. Bradman, who missed the first Test through illness, scored 396 runs at 56.57, with a century in Australia's win in the second

Test in Melbourne. Both Hammond and Sutcliffe made 440 runs at 55; Hammond made 112 in the first Test in Sydney and 101 in the fifth, also in Sydney.

Everything was overshadowed by the controversy generated by Bodyline itself. Even in the England camp it did not meet with universal approval. The amateur fast bowler, Gubby Allen, refused to bowl it. The professionals were solidly loyal to Jardine, but Hammond was one of several to express reservations about the tactic later. In the English summer of 1933 the England batsmen got a taste of their own medicine as the West Indian pace bowlers, Learie Constantine and Manny Martindale, unleashed some Bodyline of their own; Hammond had his chin sliced open by a bouncer from Martindale in the Manchester Test. He bumped into Robertson-Glasgow afterwards, and said, "Well…we began it, you know, and now you can see just a bit of what it was like. Just the luck of the game."

Before that, England had played two Tests in New Zealand, after Bodyline. Hammond gorged himself on what were admittedly very weak attacks. He scored 227 in Christchurch and then 336 not out (with 10 sixes) in Auckland. For once, he had out-Bradmanned The Don.

In 1934, normality, of a sort, was restored. There was no Larwood. Australia, as in 1930, won the series two-one. Bradman, who had a poor start to the series, made 758 runs at 94.75. Hammond, who never got going at all, made 162 at 20.25.

Hammond relaxing during the MCC tour of South Africa, 1930-31.

The 1936–37 Ashes series was one of the most dramatic of all. England were led by Allen and the side included Voce. A lot of experienced players had retired and England were not expected to do very well but they won the first two Tests, Hammond making 231 not out in the innings victory in the second Test in Sydney. Cardus said that he could not remember "…batsmanship of surer and more easeful technique than Hammond's", in that innings.

Then Bradman found form. The third Test at Melbourne was hugely affected by heavy rain which turned the pitch into a minefield. Allen declared England's first innings on 76 for nine (Hammond top scored with 32) and Bradman reversed his batting order, going in at number seven to join Fingleton on 97 for five. They put on 346 and Australia won by 365 runs.

So the fourth Test, at Adelaide, was crucial. England responded to Australia's 288 with 330. In Australia's second innings Bradman made 212, but nobody else got more than 50. England needed 392 to win. At close of play on the fourth day they were 148 for three.

Next morning, Hammond was bowled by the third ball of the day. Cardus, in the press box, overheard George Duckworth, the former England wicketkeeper: "We wouldn't have got Don out first thing in the morning with rubber at stake." Australia duly took that game and the next to win the series three-two.

On Bradman's third tour of England, in 1938, Hammond was his opposite number as captain. The series was drawn one-all; the Manchester Test was abandoned without a ball being bowled. Hammond made a majestic 240 at Lord's: his greatest Test match innings, according to Cardus. Here one saw the true grandeur of Hammond.

As Robertson-Glasgow put it: "It is something to have seen Hammond walk out to the Australians from the pavilion at Lord's; a ship in full sail."

At The Oval, Hutton's marathon enabled Hammond to declare on 903 for seven. He would have enjoyed that – especially when Bradman limped off with a twisted ankle which prevented him from batting.

He led England to successive series wins against South Africa, away (three centuries in the four Tests) and West Indies at home, hitting Test cricket's last pre-war century at The Oval.

Hammond was 42 by the time the war was over, but he had a very successful 1946, and there was no obvious alternative to lead MCC to Australia in 1946–47.

In retrospect, it was a tragic mistake. England had simply not recovered from the war. Australia won the first three games by a distance. Hammond, troubled by fibrositis and personal problems, failed. "Mentally," according to Foot, "he was in turmoil." He had just got divorced and details of this were all over the Australian newspapers. Meanwhile his second wife-to-be was very unhappy at being left in England.

The pivotal moment of the series came on the very first morning, at Brisbane. Bradman, clearly struggling, edged a ball to Jack Ikin at second slip who appeared to take a clean catch. The umpire said not out. "That's a bloody good way to start the series," observed Hammond. Bradman scored 187.

The tour ruined Hammond's reputation as a captain. But it was hardly his fault that Australia were so much better. His temperament was thought to be a problem in getting the best out of his players, certainly the young ones. The young Denis Compton was not a fan. "The players looked to the captain for guidance," he wrote, "and it wasn't there.

The only time we saw him was at the grounds." Hutton shared a car with his captain in a long journey (all car journeys are long in Australia). He was hoping for a valuable discussion; Hammond said not a word.

But Hammond cannot be held solely responsible for the failures on this tour. If anything it was the absence of young players that was the problem in 1946-47: Voce, who opened the bowling with Bedser, was 37. Years later, Hutton said Compton and Bill Edrich should have been sent home for indiscipline.

Hammond retired as soon as the tour was over. He had always been a massive force in county cricket, heading the national averages in eight successive seasons, making mountains of runs for Gloucestershire. "It's too easy," he told Cardus.

In "An Innings of Hammond," Cardus took the opportunity to complain about "utilitarian" modern batsmen – Sutcliffe, for example, and Hobbs' opening partner at Surrey, Andrew Sandham. Hammond was exempt from any such criticism. Watching an innings by Hammond, even for half an hour, your mind's eye went back to Hobbs at his finest, the pre-war Hobbs.

In his great innings against Australia at Lord's in 1938, he had come in with England in trouble with three down for 20, and "...hammered McCormick and Fleetwood-Smith and O' Reilly to shapeless helplessness." At the end of the innings there was a standing ovation, to salute a cricketer who had ennobled Lord's.

"An artist of variable moods," Cardus called him. "Perhaps all of a beautiful batsman's innings should be short," he said, recalling Edgar Allen Poe, who said that all poetry should be short. Hammond provided the rare combination of sublime artistry and statistical might. Whatever shadows cast darkness on the sunlit pathway of his career, he was a cricketing colossus.

Walter Hammond

TESTS

Batting & Fielding

M	I	NO	Runs	HS	Ave	100	50	Ct	
85	140	16	7249	336*	58.45	22	24	110	

Bowling

Balls	R	W	Ave	BBI	5W	SR	Econ	
7969	3138	83	37.80	5-36	2	96.01		

FIRST-CLASS

Batting & Fielding

M	I	NO	Runs	HS	Ave	100	50	Ct	St
634	1005	104	50551	336*	56.10	167.00	184	819	3

Bowling

Balls	R	W	Ave	BBI	5	10	Rate	
51456	22389	732	30.58	9-23	22	3	70.29	

Compton, aged 19, was picked to play against New Zealand in 1937.

5

DENIS COMPTON

Birth date	23 May 1918, died 23 April 1997
Place of birth	Hendon, Middlesex
Role	Right-handed middle-order batsman

It is not easy to do justice to Denis Compton in a way that resonates with the modern reader. His genius – this is one case where that is not too strong a word – is not easily translatable to the printed page. As John Woodcock (writing in 1998) put it, "To have a true picture of the unique charm with which Denis Compton batted at his best, it is necessary to be over fifty. This is because no one has played like him since, and there is very little vintage Compton on film that is readily available."

Jack Fingleton, who saw all the great players from the 1920s to the 1970s, said he would as soon watch a century by Compton as by any other player he had known. He was a peerless driver, said Fingleton, and a brilliant puller and hooker, showing immense courage against the sustained short-pitched bowling of the Australians in 1948. Fingleton, like many others, admired his inventiveness and ability to improvise; "He danced to his own bewitching tune," according to Woodcock. In the words of Neville Cardus, "…in point of genius he stood above all batsmen of his period. "He was unquestionably a favourite with spectators of all ages. Cardus again: "Compton's cricket was always young of impulse. He ran his runs with a most likeable waddle; when he broke his "duck" he would scamper along the pitch for dear life, as though, like any schoolboy, he was afraid he might not get another run."

His Test batting figures – 5,807 runs at an average of 50.06 – indicate that he was a batsman of the very highest class, although among the batsmen selected for this 11, he is fourth not only in the batting order but also in batting average. That said, despite what appears to have been a period of relative inflation in batting averages, no England batsman whose career extends beyond 1968 has a career average of 50 or more; Joe Root is top, and his has slid to 48. As indicated above, Compton is just behind his great contemporary, Len Hutton. Ahead of them are Jack Hobbs, Walter Hammond, Herbert Sutcliffe and Ken Barrington, of those who have played more than 20 Tests. So we are in pantheon territory here.

Consider especially Compton's extraordinary achievement in 1947, when in 50 innings in all first-class cricket, including five Tests against South Africa, he scored 3,816 runs at an average of 90.85, with 18 centuries.

Players have averaged over 100 in an English first-class season. Don Bradman and Geoff Boycott did it more than once; most famously the Australian tail-ender Bill Johnston did it in 1953 (out just once in making a season's total of 103, an achievement allegedly orchestrated by his mischief-loving captain Lindsay Hassett.) But the number of runs and centuries has never been approached and clearly never will be in first-class (red ball) cricket.

The Middlesex Twins, Bill Edrich and Denis Compton, at Lord's in 1948.

Compton playing a trademark pull to leg, 1947, his annus mirabilis.

The point is that, despite – or indeed perhaps because of – his breathtaking achievement in 1947, thinking about Compton, unlike thinking about Bradman or Boycott, does not make you think instantly about statistics. He was the complete antithesis of a "numbers man".

Mention of Hutton reminds me of a comparison that might make sense if not to the current cricket watching generation, then at least, perhaps, to the last but one. For in some ways Hutton and Compton were the Graham Gooch and David Gower of their day. Simon Wilde put it succinctly: "For Hutton cricket was always a serious business; for Compton, it was just a game."

The comparison is far from perfect but as a sort of illustrative guide it has some pointers. Gooch was the serious, almost tortured opening batsman, who as captain devised a fitness regime that was to be adhered to by everyone. Gower was the almost angelic middle-order batsman with a style that won the affection of millions but a work ethic, at least in terms of preparation, that Gooch found less than perfect.

Relations between Hutton and Compton never reached the levels of tension that marred the closing stages of Gower's Test career, but it is undoubtedly the case that there was a generally healthy rivalry between them. In his memoirs Hutton said that "[Compton's] secret was abundant natural aptitude and a gift for improvisation that amounts almost to genius." He admitted though that watching Compton's idiosyncratic sweep shot from the other end sometimes gave him a queasy stomach. This was surely inevitable. They made their Test debuts in the same series, against New Zealand, in 1937: Hutton, born in 1916, was two years older. It was immediately clear that each was an absolutely outstanding batsman. Neither took long to make his mark. Each made a century against Bradman's 1938 Australians, but of course Hutton did much more than that; his 364 at The Oval (where

Compton made one) was both a triumph and a burden. By the time cricket resumed after the 1939–45 War – what would these Titans have achieved but for that? – they were clearly the best batsmen in England and probably the world. When Hutton and Compton did well, England generally prospered. Hutton became captain, won The Ashes and got a knighthood. Compton hurt his knee, hobbled to further glories and outlasted Hutton by a couple of years. And it was Compton, not Hutton, who became a national treasure.

Like Gower, Compton was exceptionally good-looking and debonair – cricket's Prince Charming, according to Jack Fingleton. In the pre-helmet era these qualities were easily perceived by spectators. Goodness knows what sort of impact he would have made if today's social media had been available. He was a celebrity all right, but with something to be famous about. Again it was a different world in so many ways. Compton's social life, and that of his great friend and Middlesex teammate Bill Edrich (married five times, twice more than "Compo") would certainly have attracted considerable interest. His biographer, Tim Heald, recounts a story told by Fleet Street legend Reg Hayter. Hayter, while covering the 1948–49 tour of South Africa, was occasionally mistaken for Compton. One night, returning to his hotel room, he was startled to find a naked woman lying on his bed. "Hello Denis," she said," I've come to say goodnight." Her husband arrived almost immediately to drag her away.

It was Hayter who introduced Compton to Bagenal Harvey, the sports agent, who got him his famous deal with Brylcreem.

His irresistible charm and slightly chaotic lifestyle – he would frequently turn up late and have to borrow kit, including a bat, from teammates – were all part of his mystique. Above all though it was his batting, not the runs and the centuries and the average, but the style and the look of it.

Even then it is not easy to describe him. Compton was a unique combination of the conventional and the unconventional. Hutton was the classical stylist; he batted in the grand manner. Compton was the supreme entertainer. That doesn't mean he was always hitting sixes. As it happens he was a powerful batsman, with exceptionally strong forearms. But it was the versatility and unpredictability of his stroke-play that made him a joy to watch. At the same time it was universally recognised that he had a sound defensive technique. Indeed it is inconceivable that he would have made all those runs without one.

But it was the unconventionality that took the breath away. He would sometimes advance down the wicket as the bowler approached. ("I must ask him one day just why he does this," wrote Fingleton.) Or, more frequently, take his guard outside the crease. He wasn't going to be dictated to by any bowler. He had all the shots, and then some of his own invention. He made the sweep a speciality, but was both a forceful hooker and puller and the most delicate and delicious of late cutters. It was rumoured that he was not the best judge of a run.

John Arlott, in his book, Vintage Summer, about that summer of 1947, summed it up perfectly. "To close the eyes is to see again that easy, happy figure at the wicket, pushing an unruly forelock out of the eye and then, as it falls down again, playing off the wrong foot a stroke which passes deep point like a bullet...never again will the boyish delight in hitting a ball with a piece of wood flower directly into charm and gaiety and all the wealth of achievement."

Compton was born in 1918. His talent for cricket, and for football, was clear from an early age; in his teens he was on the books of both Middlesex and Arsenal. He passed a thousand runs for the season in

1936 and did even better in 1937, playing in the third and final Test against New Zealand and making 65 in the first innings. (Hutton had made a hundred in the second Test at Old Trafford.)

On his next international appearance, against Australia in the first Test of 1938, at Trent Bridge, he made 102 in the first innings. (Hutton also made a century: in fact there were four centuries in the innings.) According to Wisden, Compton's "…stylish and confident play created a big impression." In 90 minutes at the end of the first day he added 114 with Eddie Paynter. In the second Test at Lord's, a fluctuating contest, he made 76 not out in the second innings. England had made 494 (Hammond 240) and Australia 422 (Bill Brown 206 not out). England were struggling when Compton came in in the second innings and he faced a challenging attack led by the pace bowler Ernie McCormick, displaying remarkable calm for such a young player. Thanks to him England got to safety.

He missed the tour of South Africa in 1938–39, when Edrich finally established himself in the England side with a double century in the so-called Timeless Test, preferring to stay with Arsenal and further his career as one of the best outside lefts in the country.

In 1939 he scored almost 2,500 runs in first-class cricket, and made 120 in the Lord's Test against the West Indies, putting on 248 in two hours and 20 minutes with Hutton.

Then came war. Compton spent most of it in England, in various training roles in the Army; he played a number of international football matches. In 1944 he was sent to India where he played some cricket. In March 1945, the Ranji Trophy final between Bombay and Holkar produced a then record match aggregate of 2078 runs; Sergeant-Major D. C. S. Compton contributed 249 (not out) of them in Holkar's second innings.

Brothers Leslie and Denis Compton. Both played cricket for Middlesex and football for Arsenal.

He had a quiet time against India in 1946, but provided one of England's few bright spots on Hammond's tour of Australia in 1946–47. This was a difficult tour for various reasons. As in its post-World War One predecessor in 1920–21, Australia were exceptionally strong and England relatively weak. Hammond himself had a tragically difficult series, and Hutton and Compton achieved little in the first three Tests. Compton then redeemed himself making 147 and 103 not out in the fourth Test at Adelaide, in conditions of great heat and humidity.

And then came 1947. Nothing like it has happened before or since. On top of Compton's 3,816 runs, Edrich scored 3,539; both beat Tom Hayward's record that had stood since 1906. Compton's 18 hundreds beat Hobbs' record of 16 set in 1925. Middlesex duly won the county championship. In the Test matches – England won the five-match series against South Africa three-nil – Compton made 733 runs at an average of 94.12. He made 65 and 163 in the first Test at Trent Bridge, 208 in the second at Lord's (Edrich – 189 – helped him add 370 for the third wicket), 115 and 6 in the third at Old Trafford, 30 in a relatively low-scoring match at Headingley (Hutton made exactly 100) and 53 and 113 at The Oval.

In 1948 Bradman's Invincibles came to England, winning the Test series four-nil. Their formidable pace attack, led by Ray Lindwall and Keith Miller – another of Compton's lifelong friends – laid waste batting sides all around the British Isles. But Compton played two of his greatest innings in that Ashes series.

In England's second innings in the first Test at Trent Bridge he made 184, resisting Australia's attack for almost seven hours: a noble innings, said Fingleton, played in very trying conditions with frequent interruptions for bad light, and ended by a Miller bouncer which caused Compton to stumble into his stumps. Cardus called it, "One of the greatest defensive innings ever achieved in a Test match."

The third Test, in Manchester, where the England selectors caused a sensation by dropping Hutton, was the only draw. At the time the weather fatally intervened with Australia 92 for one in their second innings, chasing 317, an England win was a distinct possibility. That they were in such a position was due largely to Compton, who came in with the score on 22 for two, made a magnificent 145 not out, out of 363, in their first innings. Early in his innings, hearing a call of no ball and trying to hook, he had his forehead sliced open by a Lindwall bouncer. He resumed his innings, fortified by stitches and brandy, with the score on 119 for five and orchestrated a splendid recovery.

The fourth Test, at Headingley, is famous as the stage for one of Test cricket's greatest successful run chases, Australia making 404 for three in their second innings, with big hundreds for Bradman and opener Arthur Morris. Compton almost played a major role in this episode. He was a very useful slow left-arm bowler, purveying mostly unorthodox wrist spin – he took 622 wickets in his first-class career. Norman Yardley, England's captain, clearly thought Compton was a potent weapon in this context; he was brought on as first change before the first choice spinner, Jim Laker. And he bowled well: Godfrey Evans missed a stumping; Jack Crapp dropped Bradman. But then Morris and Bradman got after him and Yardley removed him from the attack.

Compton batting against Essex, 1946. The wicketkeeper is Tom Wade.

He scored over 1,700 runs at an average of 84 on MCC's tour of South Africa in 1948–49 and made 114 in the second Test in Johannesburg, but his most extraordinary performance was a three-hour triple century against North-East Transvaal at Benoni; the third hundred took 37 minutes.

It was around now, however, that the cricketing gods, who had smiled so benignly on Compton for so long, began to take a more jaundiced view. Because it was around this time that The Knee became a serious issue.

In the last county match of the 1947 season he had to retire hurt with a knee problem. Knee trouble had actually started before the war due to a football injury. But from 1949 it got steadily worse, becoming a matter of huge public interest so that Compton's Knee almost became detached from the individual, like Jenkins' Ear. Finally this occurred literally, in 1956, when his right kneecap was removed: the surgeon donated it to MCC.

It is probably fair to say that Compton was not quite the same player from the early 1950s. This is hardly surprising: his best had been so astonishingly good. He rarely managed a full Test series in the 1950s: the knee just did not allow it.

There were still outstanding performances. These did not include his catastrophic tour of Australia in 1950–51, when he scored 53 runs in eight innings, a mystifying failure. He averaged over 50 on the tour as a whole so it is not as if he was completely out of form. He was Freddie Brown's vice-captain, so he had extra responsibilities. The Knee was certainly an issue. He missed the second Test because of it but refused to use it as an excuse. His biographer, Ian Peebles, said it was psychological: bad luck and poor umpiring decisions (as late as 1982–83 Bob Willis joked that Australia were playing with 13 men) and repeated failures meant increasing pressure. Like most of the batsmen he struggled against mystery spinner Jack Iverson. At Melbourne, his batting partner David Sheppard called him for a mid-pitch conference. "You keep playing Iverson the way you are," Compton said, "and leave the antics to me."

Compton and Jack Robertson in 1948. Both played for Middlesex and England.

But there was genuine cause for celebration ahead. When Hutton's side regained The Ashes in 1953 after a 19-year gap, Compton hit the winning runs at The Oval; Edrich was with him at the end. He made useful contributions when Hutton retained the urn in 1954–55. He and the young Colin Cowdrey had an important partnership in the decisive game at the Adelaide Oval. Cowdrey wrote years later of how encouraging Compton had been to him; he was also struck by how nervous the veteran had been before going into bat. Meanwhile, in 1954, Compton had made his highest Test score, 278 against Pakistan at Trent Bridge. Compton himself regarded his half century in the final Test of that series at The Oval, a famous game won for Pakistan by the legendary fast-medium bowler Fazal Mahmood, as one of his best in Tests.

He had a good series against South Africa in 1955, making 492 runs at 54.66, scoring 158 at Old Trafford. The knee operation ruled him out of the first four Ashes Tests of 1956, but returned at The Oval and top scored in the first innings with 94. His international career ended with MCC's tour of South Africa in 1956–57. The following summer he retired as a professional cricketer.

At the end, we have to come back to 1947. As always, context is everything. This was "austerity Britain." The winter of 1946–47 had been bitterly cold. Everything was grey and miserable. Food was still rationed. And suddenly, in that glorious summer, the clouds lifted and the sun came out, and there he was, Denis Compton, the joyous, inimitable run scorer. And there were so many runs, and so many centuries.

Basil Easterbrook got it right in an article in the 1965 Wisden, "I see him again with the eyes of 1947, as he was at Lord's and on all the bill posters, England in a pair of pads, dark, competent, unflustered and I am glad that the most runs and most centuries concentrated into one marvellous summer will remain for all time in his keeping. For once, the gods chose right."

Denis Compton, 1936.

Denis Compton

TESTS

Batting & Fielding

M	I	NO	Runs	HS	Ave	100	50	Ct
78	131	15	5807	278	50.06	17	28	49

Bowling

Balls	R	W	Ave	BBI	5W	SR	Econ	
2716	1410	25	56.40	5-17	1	108.64		

FIRST-CLASS

Batting & Fielding

M	I	NO	Runs	HS	Ave	100	50	Ct
515	839	88	38942	300	51.85	123	182	416

Bowling

Balls	R	W	Ave	BBI	5	10	Rate	
36749	20074	622	32.27	7-36	19	3	59.08	

Stokes celebrates his first Test century, at Perth in 2013. He scored 120.

6

BEN STOKES

Birth date	4 June 1991
Place of birth	Christchurch, New Zealand
Role	All-rounder. Left-handed middle-order batsman, right arm fast-medium bowler

Ben Stokes is a star in all formats. The principal benchmark for inclusion in this book has been sustained success against the top sides in Test cricket. By 28 he had played 57 Tests averaging 35 with the bat and 32 with the ball; that's what you want from your all-rounder.

Stokes compares favourably with the other great post-war English all-rounders: Flintoff, 31 and 33, Ian Botham, 33 and 28, Tony Greig, 40 and 32, and Trevor Bailey, 29 and 29. All these players were outstanding in their very different ways. But none of them, not even Botham, achieved highs – and lows – in the sensational way that Stokes has managed.

An all-rounder naturally has more opportunities to affect the course of a match than a specialist batsman or bowler.

If that all-rounder is also a brilliant fielder, the opportunities for a decisive intervention seem almost limitless. Andrew "Freddy" Flintoff, England's last great all-rounder before Stokes, played a decisive role in some epic struggles against Australia, especially in 2005, but nobody who saw it will forget his running out of Ricky Ponting to secure England's win at The Oval in 2009. It came out of nowhere – poor old Fred had seemed barely mobile at times. But he just wouldn't keep quiet; he was compelled to make things happen. Such players are not common. Stokes is one of them.

Even five-day diehards have to admit that England's greatest achievement in recent years was becoming World Cup champions in 2019. Stokes was the key performer; his batting average of 66.42, strike rate of 93.18, and economy with the ball of 4.83, speak volumes.

He made an immediate impact on the tournament as England overwhelmed South Africa at The Oval. Stokes made 89 off 79 balls, with only nine boundaries, and took two wickets in two overs to finish the match. But his most memorable contribution was an amazing running, diving catch on the boundary to dismiss Andile Phehlukwayo. The ball appeared to be not sailing but speeding over the midwicket boundary as Stokes raced after it, leapt, caught it one-handed and clung on as he fell. That is the sort of thing Stokes does. He makes things happen, whatever he is doing.

He produced consistent performances throughout, none more impressive, in its way, than his 82 not out (seven fours and four sixes) in the defeat to Sri Lanka at Headingley. This was a game which, at the halfway stage, no serious judge thought England could lose, but gormless batting ensued. Only Stokes was exempt from criticism. If somebody – anybody – could have stayed with him for a few overs, they would have won.

Then there was the final, at Lord's, against New Zealand. In this wonderful cricket match the tension grew to an almost unbearable level as England pursued, rather painfully, their target of 242. When Stokes and Jos Buttler were putting on 110 for the fifth wicket it looked as though they were going to get there. It was Buttler's departure, to a brilliant catch by substitute Tim Southee, which led to the final climactic events.

This time Stokes made 84 not out off 98 balls (five fours and two sixes – there were only four in the match). An extraordinary innings culminating in the most dramatic finale, with 15 required to win off the last over, bowled by Trent Boult. The first two balls Stokes hit hard but straight to fielders; a run was possible, certainly off the first one but Stokes chose not to take one. When the third ball came, you could see why; Stokes took a big stride and slog swept magnificently for six: now it was nine off three. At this point fate took a hand. Stokes smashed the fourth ball square on the leg side. He and his partner, Adil Rashid, had to run and they had to run two. As Stokes dived to make ground, his outstretched bat collided with the returned ball, which sped to the untenanted boundary behind the wicketkeeper. Now it was three off two.

In some ways the final two balls were the most remarkable. Stokes made one off each, his partner being run out going for the second each time. For Stokes this wasn't a death or glory situation. He was immensely cool and showed a remarkably shrewd cricket brain to go for the super-over, and second chance.

And then there was Headingley and the Ashes miracle. As the World Cup had reached its finale, New Zealand definitely looked like favourites but at Headingley in the third Ashes Test just six weeks later, England were bowled-out for 67 in their first innings, with Stokes himself out for eight to an unsightly swish off James Pattinson.

That England were not totally out of the match was down to their bowlers, and in particular to Stokes who bowled a magnificent and incisive spell on the second afternoon to ensure that nobody was going to hang around too long with the adhesive Marnus Labuschagne. Stokes, who dismissed Travis Head, Matthew Wade and Pat Cummins, finished with figures of three for 56 off 22.4 overs, and with an economy rate better than any England bowler except Stuart Broad in the first innings.

When he joined Joe Root on the third afternoon the score was 141 for three. Stokes scored just two runs off his first 66 balls and his fifty was his slowest in Tests. But he was still there, with Root, when play resumed on the Sunday.

Sections of the media were quick to dub Ben Stoke's 120 in Perth in 2013 the most significant century this decade.

Most people thought the odds of an England win were somewhere between impossible and highly improbable. Critical would be the first hour and, in particular, the new ball, due after seven overs. But if the not-out pair could survive till lunch, well, who knew what might happen.

The day started in glorious sunshine but strange almost sepulchral silence from a capacity crowd. We didn't have to wait long. Root fell almost at once to Nathan Lyon. No runs came in the first five overs. But Jonny Bairstow, one Yorkshire man replacing another, got things moving and that pair were still there at lunch: 238 for four.

After lunch though there was another of those apparently seismic shifts. Tim Paine's go-to men, Nathan Lyon and Josh Hazlewood, applied pressure and England faltered. Bairstow edged to second slip, Buttler was run out in a mix-up with Stokes and Chris Woakes was undone by some short stuff. Jofra Archer hung around but when he and Broad were out to successive balls, it was 286 for nine (Stokes 61 off 174 balls), with 73 needed – Stokes and Jack Leach would have to get them.

And they did. Well, Leach got one, the single that brought the scores level. But he played his part all right: Jack Leach, Ashes hero.

It is hard to know where to begin with Stokes. He finished on 135 not out, with eleven fours and eight sixes, and made 74 of the tenth wicket partnership of 76. It is almost as if he knew, right from the start of his innings, that England were going to win and that he was going to win it for them. His early self-denial was startling in its intensity. It was as though his first innings dismissal – a crass swipe at a ball that was virtually a wide – was endlessly replaying in his mind.

Once he was joined by Leach there was only one way he could go. And he went. Eight sixes and eleven fours, mostly in that last, epic partnership. From a no-risk game it became an all-risk game. Paine, increasingly flummoxed, spread the field far and wide. Stokes was simply too smart for his eleven opponents. He kept taking them on, and winning, farming the strike and hitting whenever possible. The shot of the day? It's really impossible to choose, but perhaps the incredible reverse slog sweep for six off Lyon.

Yes Lyon, the best finger spinner in the world; Pat Cummins, the world's number one ranked bowler; Hazlewood, the best bowler in the match – he conceded 19 in an over near the end; Pattinson, still firing down 90 mph deliveries at both batsmen. They had carried all before them in the series, like Dennis Lillee and Terry Alderman in 1981. Now on this crazy sunlit afternoon, control eluded them.

A one-wicket victory in a tight series is always going to be special. Although one inevitably thinks of Headingley 1981, the more comparable match situations were Melbourne 1982–83 and Edgbaston 2005. But neither of those had an individual performance to rank with Stokes' historic series and career defining innings. One man, against eleven desperadoes. Paine's men more or less fell apart by the end. Yes they were under pressure but who was under more pressure? The Australians' gormless use of the review system could have cost them the Ashes (although the series was squared in the end).

Every one of the (largely) exultant spectators, and the thousands watching on television, would have been struggling to nominate a greater innings. There have been only 14 one-wicket wins in over 2,000 Tests. The thirteenth was just a few months earlier when Sri Lanka's Kusal Perera and Vishwa Fernando put on an unbroken 78 for the tenth wicket to win the first Test against South Africa at Durban by one wicket.

Perera made 153 not out, with 12 fours and five sixes. Theirs is the highest ever tenth wicket partnership to win a Test match.

There is one other obvious comparison. The third Test between the West Indies and Australia at Bridgetown in 1998–99 was a must-win game for the hosts and their captain, Brian Lara. Australia had a first innings lead of 161 but were bowled out for 146 in their second innings. West Indies won, making 311 for nine; Lara made 153 not out.

Stokes' innings was remarkably similar to Perera's in a number of ways, but the context of an Ashes series hanging in the balance probably gives him the edge. The fact that we can speak about Stokes (and Perera for that matter) in the same breath as Lara, undoubtedly one of the greatest batsmen of the modern era, is testament to the achievement.

It was Stokes' second Ashes century in successive matches and his second successive match award. His 115 not out in the drawn second Test at Lord's was a brilliant innings, again having a transformative impact on the game and giving England a real and unexpected chance of victory.

Playing a key role in Ashes series victories is a recurring theme in this book and Stokes has played his part. England won the 2015 series three-two, winning the third Test at Trent Bridge by eight wickets. Stuart Broad took eight for 15 on the first morning, as Australia were bowled out for 60. The catch that Stokes, at fifth – yes, fifth – slip, took to dismiss Adam Voges was, literally, incredible. The ball seemed to have sped past his right hand as he dived but he somehow clung on to it. Then in Australia's second innings he took six for 36 with high-quality pace and swing, coming on when Australia had reached 113 for no wicket and removing Chris Rogers, David Warner and Shaun Marsh in successive overs.

He was triumphant at Lord's earlier in the year when England won a classic game against New Zealand by 122 runs. England, inserted by Brendon McCullum, endured a "here we go again" start and were 31 for four after thirteen overs with their most experienced batsmen, captain Alastair Cook and Ian Bell, among those back in the hutch. But a sterling revival was led by the increasingly dependable Root and rising star Stokes. They had already put on fifty by lunch and played with increasing authority through the afternoon. Both narrowly missed centuries – Stokes made 92 from 94 balls – but the good work was carried on by Buttler and Moeen Ali. England's eventual total of 389 seemed more than respectable.

It was put in perspective, though, by New Zealand's reply. While England's top four made 1, 16, 1 and 1, New Zealand's contributed 70, 59, 132 and 62. When play ended on the second day with the Kiwis on 303 for two, with Kane Williamson on 92 and Ross Taylor on 47, there seemed to be only one side in it.

Posting runs against Mitchell Johnson on his home wicket at the WACA.

New Zealand reached 523, and though the lead of 132 was substantial enough it represented something of a clawback by England.

Their second innings started with Southee and Boult again on target, with England 25 for two in the eighth over. Cook and Bell got them through to stumps. The fourth morning was going to be critical.

Bell was out to the third ball of the day. Conditions were as favourable to the bowlers as at any time in the match but Cook and Root stood firm and prospered, putting on a critical 158 for the fourth wicket, before Root fell for 84 with the score on 232, a lead of 98.

The match was won, and lost, on the fourth afternoon. It was one of those occasions, not uncommon in Test cricket, when the taking of a new ball proves decisive – in favour of the batting side.

When Southee took the new ball with England on 269 for four, Cook was on 106 and Stokes had made 29 off 36 balls. That was after 80 overs. By the time Stokes was out, for 101 in the 95th over, off 92 balls, the score was 364 for five and the game had been transformed. This time Stokes made the second fastest Test century ever by an England batsman, taking just 85 balls (the fastest ever in a Test at Lord's). And he wasn't done yet. New Zealand's target was 345 in 77 overs. A successful run chase was highly unlikely, although New Zealand had made a Test-record run-rate of 4.92 to win the second Test at Headingley. Stokes dismissed their two most dangerous batsmen, Williamson and McCullum, with successive balls. At one point his figures were three overs, two for none.

Others may take more wickets – Broad, and James Anderson in particular – but Stokes is the ultimate "go to" bowler. The first Test against India at Edgbaston in August 2018 was another gripping contest, which England won by 31 runs. India's target was 194, and they started the final morning on 110 for five. But their captain Virat Kohli, who had made a masterly 149 in the first innings, was in. The score crept up and then accelerated. With 51 needed, Root brought

Stokes back and in his first over he dismissed Kohli leg before. Three balls later he had Mohammed Shami caught behind; the end was nigh.

As things stand, Stokes' batting seems the stronger suit. An orthodox left-hander, he is sound in defence, and utterly destructive in attack. He is a thoroughly modern batsman; he has taken the best of T20 and adapted it for the five-day game. This could be seen clearly at Headingley, where slog-sweeps and ramp shots kept company with powerful drives and cuts. The power of his strokes is awe-inspiring. But he is still capable of losing the plot. In the first Test against New Zealand at Mount Maunganui in November 2019 he batted beautifully to reach 92 and then rushed down the wicket to a ball from Southee, had a swing and was caught at slip. A predictable collapse ensued and an apparently promising position was sacrificed; England ended up losing by an innings.

His right-arm pace bowling has been clocked at 140kph and he often finds more swing than anyone else; six for 22 against West Indies in the Lord's Test in 2017 was a classic example. And his stamina is tremendous.

Stokes was born in Christchurch, New Zealand. His father was a rugby league player and coach. They moved to England when Ben was twelve. He quickly established himself when he joined Durham and was soon selected for the England Lions. Then he got picked for the (catastrophic) Ashes tour of 2013–14. Although Stokes made a fighting century in the third Test at Perth and took six for a costly 99 off 19 in the final Test in Sydney, he subsequently lost his Test place and, incredible though it now seems, was dropped for the disastrous World Cup campaign of 2015. But his performances against New Zealand and Australia that summer marked him out as one to watch.

Nobody could have anticipated his impact on the first two days of England's Test against South Africa at Cape Town in January 2016.

Coming in at number six with Kagiso Rabada on a hat-trick, he scored an astonishing 258 off 196 balls, the fastest 250 ever in a Test. On the second morning he moved from 74 to 204, the most anyone has made in the morning session. He and fellow redhead Bairstow put on 399 in 366 minutes, the highest ever sixth-wicket Test partnership.

The triumph of the 2019 World Cup was all the sweeter because of previous short format near misses. England looked good enough to beat anyone in the Champions Trophy they hosted in 2017 but were undone by Pakistan in the semi-final in Cardiff, managing only 211 in their 49.5 overs. Stokes made 34 from 94 balls. "So often England's heartbeat," wrote Lawrence Booth, "Stokes batted as if he'd had a transplant."

And then there was the World T20 Championship in India in March/April 2016. The final between England and West Indies, in Eden Gardens, Kolkata (one of the game's great theatres) came down to the last over. West Indies needed 19 to win. Their best player, Marlon Samuels, was 85 not out, but was at the wrong end. Facing was Carlos Brathwaite, who had only faced 18 balls in the tournament before this match. And the bowler was Stokes, England's specialist at the death.

Like so many things about Stokes, it was barely credible. Four balls, four sixes, game over. Poor Stokes. Surely he was thinking about this as he put his arm round Jofra Archer's shoulder before the super-over at Lord's in 2019.

We keep coming back to the World Cup. England wouldn't have won it without Stokes. Would they have lost the 2017–18 Ashes with him?

He had a great 2017 against South Africa and West Indies. The end of the season saw a one-day series against West Indies. On the night after the third game, at Bristol, Stokes was involved in a fracas outside a nightclub. The incident was, inevitably, captured on a mobile phone, leaked to the media, and has probably been seen by at least the same number of people who watched the closing overs of the World Cup.

Stokes' 2017–18 Ashes ended there and then. He was charged with affray, eventually acquitted at trial, but in the interim, the cricketing authorities had no choice but to make an example of this so-called role model and England vice-captain.

But 2019 was the year of redemption in cricket. Steve Smith, disgraced sandpaper overseer, batted like Bradman, and was booed through the length and breadth of the United Kingdom, until finally, at The Oval, out for 23 – caught by Stokes – he got the standing ovation he deserved.

And Stokes? His wonderful hundred at Lord's was his first since Bristol. From the start of the World Cup he was his old self, only more so. He had had disciplinary issues before – he was sent home early from the 2012–13 Lions tour of Australia – but he seemed exceptionally well behaved now. And why shouldn't he be? For a while he must have thought it could be all over.

Watching him in the field now, he has leader written all over him. His reading of situations is second to none. Whether, after Bristol, captaincy is even a theoretical possibility is one of the main questions facing English cricket.

Whatever happens, we're not going to stop watching, and talking about, Ben Stokes, "England's heartbeat."

Ben Stokes

TESTS

Batting & Fielding

M	I	NO	Runs	HS	Ave	100	50	Ct	
59	108	4	3738	258	35.94	8	20	60	

Bowling

Balls	R	W	Ave	BBI	5	10	SR	Econ	
8217	4584	137	33.45	6–22	4	0	59.9	3.34	

ONE-DAY INTERNATIONALS

Batting & Fielding

M	I	NO	Runs	HS	Ave	SR	100	50	Ct
95	81	15	2682	102*	40.63	93.94	3	20	45

Bowling

Balls	R	W	Ave	BBI	5	SR	Econ	
2912	2920	70	41.71	5–61	1	41.60	6.01	

FIRST-CLASS

Batting & Fielding

M	I	NO	Runs	HS	Ave	100	50	Ct	
135	229	12	7531	258	34.70	16	39	101	

Bowling

Balls	R	W	Ave	BBI	5	10	SR	Econ	
16104	9333	309	30.2	7–67	7	1	52.10	3.47	

Ian Botham in 1975, in the early stages of his career with Somerset.

7

IAN BOTHAM

Birth date	24 November 1955
Place of birth	Heswall, Cheshire
Role	Right-handed middle-order batsman, right-arm fast-medium bowler

Who is the most popular, and most deified, of all England cricketers? Even with all the excitement of the 2019 Men's World Cup and the heroics of Ben Stokes, and Andrew Flintoff's triumph in the 2005 Ashes – the last time England's cricketers could be seen on free-to-air television – it would be a brave judge who gave any name other than Ian Botham.

The reason is a few weeks of extraordinary cricket in the summer of 1981, when Botham was 25 years old. It was an Ashes summer, and England were the holders.

By this time Botham was certainly one of the best cricketers in the world. Ultimately of course his Test record speaks for itself. He scored 14 hundreds, took 383 wickets, and held

120 catches, most of them in the slips. He took 21 Tests to reach the double of 1,000 runs and 100 wickets, 27 fewer than Gary Sobers and nine fewer than Imran Khan. But the people who remember Botham the cricketer don't remember any of that. They remember a larger than life personality, aggressive and confident in everything he did. They remember enthusiasm and conviction, booming straight drives, violent hooks and pulls, and mischievous reverse sweeps. They remember, in his pomp, according to Tony Lewis, "the aggression in his personality did much to make him the most dangerous attacking player in the world, an all-rounder capable of swinging the outcome of Test matches by his own performance." And they remember a bowler who was always "in the face" of the batsman. In his pomp, between 1977 and 1981, he was, according to Mike Brearley (writing in 2018), with his pace and his swing, a better bowler than any of his three great all-rounder contemporaries, Imran Khan, Kapil Dev and Richard Hadlee.

Cricket had gone through a turbulent period because of the so-called "Packer revolution" which had split global cricket in the late 1970s. The controversy related to the ambition of the Australian television magnate Kerry Packer to secure the rights to broadcast Australian Test cricket. When the Australian board refused to talk, Packer hired many of the world's best players and set up a rival "circus" to compete with the official game.

This process was in its early stages during Australia's tour of England in 1977, when Botham made his Test debut. Not surprisingly, Australia were more seriously affected than any other team by the Packer turmoil, and it was a somewhat disconsolate side that Greg Chappell led to England.

England themselves were hardly unaffected. Their charismatic captain, Tony Greig, turned out to have been Packer's ace recruiter, and he was stripped of the captaincy, though he remained in the team for the 1977 series. He was replaced as captain by the cerebral opening batsman, Brearley.

Botham pushing for a quick single on the leg side.

Brearley led England to victory in that Ashes series, and to an even more emphatic win Down Under in 1978–79, by which time Packer's depredations had had an even more critical impact on the Australian squad. A year later, an exhausted truce was called. Packer basically got what he wanted. A full Australian side thrashed Brearley's England in 1979–80, but the Ashes were not at stake. (Every series since 1882 played between England and Australia has been fought over the Ashes, sport's smallest trophy but one of its most venerable and intriguing. The urn is kept in a glass case in the museum at Lord's, although at the time of writing it is about to make one of its rare trips to Australia, on its own business class seat. The England cricket authorities were prepared, as a gesture of goodwill, to play three Tests in 1979–80 but not to recognise them as constituting a contest for the Ashes.)

The big change for England when Kim Hughes' Australians turned up for the 1981 Ashes was that there was a new captain: Botham. Was it inevitable that Botham would become England captain? Probably yes. Brearley had made it clear he didn't want to tour again, so a change was going to have to be made.

There was no doubt that Botham was the best player in the side. And he was in outstanding form. In the third Test against Australia at Sydney in 1979–80 he had made a brilliant second-innings century, coming in at 88 for five and batting with the tail. Then came the Golden Jubilee Test against India in Bombay (Mumbai) in February 1980.

This match saw a truly epic performance by England's all-rounder. It was a game between two exhausted teams and was not of the highest quality but at least Botham ensured that it would never be forgotten.

India, winning the toss, struggled to 242, with Botham taking six for 58. England were soon in trouble at 58 for five but Botham added 171 with Bob Taylor. Botham scored 114, and England made 296. Second time around India could make only 149: Botham took seven for 48. England won by 10 wickets.

Early in the domestic season he made his highest first-class score, 228, for Somerset against Gloucestershire at Taunton, with 10 sixes and 27 fours. So he was full of confidence too.

Geoff Lawson is hit by Botham bouncer at Headingley, 1985.

Brearley, a shrewd judge, has made it very clear that he thought Botham was the right choice. He did think, however, that the selectors could have retained him as captain for the first couple of Tests in the summer of 1980, so as to ease Botham into the job. But Brearley admired Botham's "natural feel for the game," his tactical astuteness and leadership qualities. One dissenting voice, acknowledged by Botham in his autobiography, was his most valued mentor in cricket, Brian Close, his first captain at Somerset. Close thought he was too young, at 24, and too naive to deal with the man-management side of the job.

Timing of course is everything. Botham's record as England's Test captain is underwhelming: played 12, won none, drew eight, lost four. But who was he playing? He only had two opponents – the West Indies and Australia.

The West Indies were just about at the height of their powers when Botham's England side took them on in successive series in 1980, in England and 1980–81 in the Caribbean. The visitors won the first Test in 1980 and the rest were drawn. The weather often interrupted play.

The series in the Caribbean was much more challenging. The pace attack, comprising Andy Roberts, Michael Holding, Colin Croft and Joel Garner, was, as ever, relentless, and there were off-field challenges for a young captain to deal with, notably the political brouhaha ignited by the selection of Robin Jackman to join the tour party, which led to the cancellation of the Test in Guyana due to Jackman's South African connections, and the tragic death of the much-loved assistant manager Ken Barrington. Altogether, especially given results against the same opposition later in the decade, two-nil wasn't so bad.

In between those two series England played the Centenary Test against Australia at Lord's, another rain-affected draw.

And then there was the Ashes of 1981, the first official contest since Packer. A little gloss was taken off by the fact that Australia's best player, Greg Chappell, had opted not to tour, and ace fast bowler Jeff Thomson was also missing, the selectors preferring the rookie Terry Alderman, whose swing bowling, it was thought, would suit English conditions.

The tourists didn't win a first-class match before the first Test at Trent Bridge, but they did win the three-match one-day series two-one, and to some astonishment they won that Test, a riveting and unpredictable affair, by four wickets. The dominant figures were Australia's new-ball pairing,

Alderman and Dennis Lillee, who shared 17 wickets between them. England's 185 in their first innings was the highest score of the match.

Botham shares a joke with the umpire whilst receiving treatment for a foot injury during the sixth Ashes Test at The Oval in 1985.

So there was pressure on the young England captain going into the second Test at Lord's. Neither side was able to wrestle an advantage but the match was a deeply unhappy one for Botham, who bagged a pair and, after his second dismissal walked through the famous old Long Room in the great Pavilion to a "pointed silence" (Brearley's phrase) from the members. He resigned the captaincy. (Chairman of selectors Alec Bedser helpfully let it be known that they would have sacked him.)

The real problem with Botham's captaincy wasn't the results so much as his own loss of form. In those twelve matches he scored one fifty and took no five-wicket hauls. Botham himself has always maintained that the loss of form was a coincidence. He never had the chance to find out.

Brearley came back as captain for the third Test at Headingley.

This game is extremely well known and the events barely need to be recounted. It is one of only three Tests – one in each century in which Test cricket has been played – in which a side won the game after being required to follow on. That side was England, and England won because of one man – Ian Botham.

Australia made 401 in their first innings, Botham taking six for 95 in 38 overs. It was during this innings that Brearley, noticing that Botham was running in more slowly than before and incorporating a small kink in his final approach, started referring to his star all-rounder as the "sidestep queen."

England were then dismissed for 174 (Botham 50) by Alderman, Lillee and Geoff Lawson. Following on, they immediately lost Graham Gooch. Rain and bad light prevented further mishap on that day, the third. The following day, Sunday, was a rest day.

In Brearley's words, "[t]he last two days of the Headingley Test were the most extraordinary and unbelievable that most of us have witnessed."

England lost wickets steadily to Alderman and Lillee on Monday; at around 3 pm, when Graham Dilley joined Botham, the score was 135 for seven, with England still 92 behind.

Nobody would say that Botham's innings of 149 not out was a technical masterpiece. Brearley was probably closer to the truth when, after the game he referred to it as "pure village green stuff." In Botham's own words, far from being a carefully planned assault, "it was just one of those crazy, glorious one-off flukes." In a sense he followed Dilley's lead in deciding to have a swing and see what happened. If it was short, he hooked, pulled or cut; if full, he drove. There was no science to it. Twenty-seven fours. One six, a glorious straight drive off Alderman. Alderman and Lillee, who had carried all before them, in the match and the series, were run ragged. Dilley, who made 56, helped Botham add 117 in 80 minutes. Botham moved on to his hundred (off 87 balls) and added 67 with Chris Old for the ninth wicket. At close of play the score was 351 for nine, 124 ahead.

It had been a transformative session of play. The most obvious and immediate impact was on the match itself. Until quite late on that fourth afternoon everyone assumed England would lose. A number of England players, including Botham, had checked out of the team hotel; Brearley hadn't, but only because Middlesex had a county game starting at Old Trafford on the Wednesday. By the end of the day things looked different. Australia's eventual target was 130, easily the smallest total of the match. But the psychological flow of the match had changed completely. At one stage Australia were 58 for two. A rampaging Bob Willis (eight for 43) drove England home; but without Botham they would never have got there.

The other transformation, as significant in its way as the impact on the match, was that of Botham himself. It was more than the simple reaffirmation of him as the world's leading all-rounder, after a year or more of under-achievement, though that was special enough. But Botham was now more than that: he was a superstar. Two of his contemporaries, his long-term Somerset team mate Vic Marks, and his occasional England teammate Derek Pringle, have recently written that Botham, in the early 1980s, was easily, incomparably, the most famous sportsman in England, far more famous than any footballer. That must seem staggering to anyone living in England now. It puts Botham, in terms of fame, right up there with Denis Compton, W. G. Grace even. And he was just 25.

Reverting to the purely cricketing consequences, Headingley (and what followed) gave Botham a hold over the Australians – the old enemy – that was to last for the best part of a decade. But he wasn't finished with the 1981 lot yet.

The fourth Test was at Edgbaston. It was another remarkable low scoring game. No batsman reached fifty.

Brearley won the toss and chose to bat. England made 189 (Alderman five for 42). Australia made 258, and then bowled England out for 219 (Ray Bright five for 68).

Another of those intriguing targets: 150. At 87 for three, then 105 for four, it looked as though Australia would get there. Allan Border was out on that score and Brearley put Botham on, with instructions to "keep things tight" for John Emburey.

As Brearley admitted, Botham did that all right; in his spell of 28 balls he conceded just one run. And he took five wickets – Australia, all out for 121, lost by 29 runs; Botham 14-9-11-5. The last five wickets went for seven runs. It was mainly pace that did it. Rod Marsh, Martin Kent and Alderman were bowled, Bright leg before and Lillee caught behind.

It was two-one to England with two to play when the teams convened at Old Trafford, so the Ashes were still in play.

Brearley again won the toss, and England made 231 (Chris Tavare 69, four wickets each to Lillee and Alderman.) Australia made only 130 (Willis four for 63, Botham three for 28.) England were batting again by 4 pm on the second day.

At the start of the third day England seemed well placed, 171 ahead with nine second innings wickets standing. But Australia fought back in the morning taking four wickets for only 34 runs. Tavare scored nine in the two hours before lunch. He was joined by Botham after lunch with the score 104 for five.

Tony Lewis said of Botham (seen here in 1980), "the aggression in his personality did much to make him the most dangerous attacking player in the world, an all-rounder capable of swinging the outcome of Test matches by his own performance."

This innings of 118 was even better than the Headingley one. Brearley called it "an innings of classical power and splendour." Whereas at Headingley he had been almost literally chancing his arm from beginning to end, this was a Test match innings of polished grandeur rather than brute strength. He played himself in properly and applied a degree of, if not caution, then at least reasonable circumspection, even though the innings lasted little longer than a session. There was nothing bucolic about the strokeplay (six sixes and 13 fours); this was batsmanship of the highest order. Perhaps there was an element of the essential, muscular "Beefy" too; Brearley called it, "an innings of unusually cultured brutality."

Botham (and Tavare, 78 in seven hours, all the circumspection you need) put the game out of Australia's reach. At one point they took 22 off an over from Lillee (Botham 19, Tavare 3). Despite centuries from Allan Border and Graham Yallop, Australia were never in the hunt. Near the end, Botham took a glorious leaping slip catch to dismiss Lillee. England won by 103 runs, and thus retained the Ashes: Botham's Ashes.

It was always clear he was going to be something special. Born in Cheshire but growing up in Yeovil, Somerset. He spent time on the MCC groundstaff before joining the county on the same day, in 1974, as Marks, Viv Richards and Peter Roebuck.

He made an immediate mark. In June 1974, playing in a quarter-final against Hampshire, he bowled Hampshire's opening batsman, Barry Richards, one of the best batsmen in the world. Then, when Hampshire seemed to have the game sewn up, Botham showed great courage against fast bowler Andy Roberts, who knocked out two of his teeth with a bouncer. Botham refused to give in. He resisted with the tail and took his team to an improbable victory.

In the 1976 season he scored over a thousand first-class runs and took 88 wickets; an international call-up could not be far away.

It came in The Ashes summer of 1977. By this time Botham was a magnificent physical specimen, big and strong, and a wonderful athlete. He also had, as that performance against Hampshire showed, unquenchable self-belief. That never changed; everything else, of course, gradually did.

He was a true all-rounder, worth his place as batsman or bowler, not to mention being an outstanding fielder, especially in the slips. On five occasions in Test cricket he hit a century and took five wickets in an innings; nobody else has done it more than twice. If I had to choose, I would probably have to say that bowling was, marginally, his stronger suit. It's difficult because he was such a supremely entertaining batsman. And it is hard to credit that the man who for a number of years was the world's leading wicket taker in Test history also hit fourteen Test match hundreds. But his arsenal as a bowler when he was at the height of his powers – pace, accuracy and the ability to move the ball both ways – probably carries the day. Above all he had the priceless gift of taking wickets. That sounds silly but it's true. Even late in his career – and Botham's powers started waning long before his career actually ended – he still had the knack of taking wickets, almost by effort of will. He didn't have to be bowling particularly well. It was like the classic partnership breaker, Basil D'Oliveira, say, or Paul Collingwood. He would trundle in and bowl and, well, there's another wicket.

It was certainly as a bowler that he made an impact in 1977. He played in two Tests, the third at Trent Bridge and the fourth at Headingley. England won both, and Botham got a five-wicket haul in each; the Aussies weren't going to forget this fellow in a hurry. That winter he made his first Test hundred, against New Zealand at Christchurch, and took five for 73 in New Zealand's first innings: England won by 174 runs. (It was in this game that he famously ran Geoffrey Boycott out for slow scoring.) In 1978 he scored a century (his second in the series) and took eight for 34 against Pakistan at Lord's.

In a sense Botham – and his great contemporary David Gower – was lucky to start his Test career when he did because so many opposing teams, like Australia and Pakistan, had their Test teams denuded by Packer. But the players have to perform against whoever they come up against. The young Botham was a giant fit to rank with the greats of any age. By his nineteenth Test, in 1979, he had reached 100 Test wickets, one of the quickest to reach that landmark.

Was it realistic to expect him to keep performing at the level of brilliance displayed in 1981? Probably not. As a "celebrity" the demands on him were bound to become more exacting. If he was fit – and for a long time he was certainly fit enough to play, although an apparently minor back injury, sustained in a game at Oxford as early as 1980, had serious long-term repercussions – he would be picked for England, summer or winter. He was also a massive contributor to Somerset's success in domestic cricket in the early 1980s. (Today's mollycoddled centrally contracted heroes have no idea.) The day after the Headingley Test of 1981 ended, for instance, the England players had to play one-day Gillette Cup matches for their counties. From his debut in 1977 he really had no time off until he opted out of Gower's tour of India in 1984–85.

In the immediate aftermath of 1981, nothing seemed to have changed. On Keith Fletcher's challenging tour of India in 1981–82 he topped the batting averages (40 runs at 55) and was England's leading wicket taker. He was in unstoppable form with the bat when India toured England in 1982, scoring 128 in the second Test at Old Trafford and then a massive and exhilarating 208 in the third at The Oval.

If there is what one could call a gap in his CV, it is his record against the West Indies. He never scored a century against them. He did take eight wickets against them, at Lord's in 1984, but this was the famous game that West Indies won by nine wickets after being set 350 on the fifth day. Like Gower, Botham was an "ever-present" in two series "blackwashes."

For Botham there was a special allure about Australia. It is one of a number of things that make one want to compare him with Shane Warne. After Warne bowled his celebrated "ball of the century" to Mike Gatting in 1993, he exerted a hold over English batsmen that he did not release until he retired 14 years later. Botham's power over Australia's players, especially after 1981, was not dissimilar. He had an uneven, slightly underwhelming time on Bob Willis' unsuccessful tour of 1982–83. But he enjoyed himself mightily when Gower won the urn back from a disconsolate Border in 1985, hitting sixes almost at will. More serious, and more impressive, was his contribution to Mike Gatting's Ashes retaining triumph in 1986–87.

This was a series England were widely expected to lose. In fact, they asserted their dominance right from the start, trouncing the hosts in the first Test at Brisbane. Botham's role in this process was vital; on the second day he pulverised the Australian attack with a forthright 138 off 114 balls, including four sixes – all straight drives – and 13 fours; one Merv Hughes over went for 22.

However, injury problems, particularly to his back (but also fair wear and tear, and a failure to take proper care of himself – he was allergic to training) meant he was no longer quite the same force with the ball; essentially he was military medium. But in the decisive fourth Test at Melbourne he helped Gladstone Small bowl England to victory with five for 41 in the first innings.

He missed part of the previous domestic season, 1986, having been banned after admitting to previous involvement with recreational drugs. He returned to the Test side for the third (drawn) game against New Zealand at The Oval. It was pure Botham theatre. The visitors batted first. After a spell from the opening bowlers, Gatting threw him the ball. With his first delivery he had Bruce Edgar caught by Gooch at slip. "Who writes your scripts?" Gooch famously asked. That took his number of Test wickets to 355, equal with Lillee. At the end of his next over he surpassed the great Australian. When he batted he made 59, reaching 50 off 32 balls including 24 from an over from David Stirling and 17 off one from Richard Hadlee.

Performances such as this inevitably became rarer and as his fitness declined he gradually departed from the international scene. There was almost a last hurrah. He was a valuable member of Gooch's World Cup squad in 1992–93, bowling some economical spells and opening the batting with Gooch in the later rounds, including the final. But it was not to be.

By this time he was no longer a Somerset player. A vitriolic row with new captain Roebuck about the sacking of overseas players Richards and Joel Garner, led to Botham's departure. This episode, which caused deep and long-lasting wounds, certainly indicated Botham's intense loyalty to his friends. He joined Worcestershire, whom he immediately helped win two county championship titles, in 1988 and 1989. He finished up with Durham, and he is now their chairman.

After 1981 he was on the front pages as often as on the back. Botham didn't always make the right decisions, but on the whole he has been a force for good. Often for the really good. His walks, to raise money for leukaemia research, have raised many millions of pounds. To see him on one of these walks, as I have, is to see a true force of nature at work. He starts at the crack of dawn, and he walks and walks; normal people have to run to keep up. It's party time in the evening and then he walks again.

Paul Downton and Geoff Miller congratulate Ian Botham after he trapped Vivian Richards for 72 in the first innings of the Lord's Test against West Indies in 1984. Captain David Gower looks on thoughtfully, as well he might. Botham took eight wickets in that innings but West Indies won the match by nine wickets after an extraordinary fifth day run chase.

He was a fixture on Sky for years. He was not a natural pundit. But he had a good cricket brain and, as he would never hesitate to point out, the great merit of always being right.

And yes, he remains immensely popular. And you can see why. Reading Marks' memoirs one of the aspects which stands out is the number of understated acts of kindness from Botham: little, nameless, unremembered acts. Although the former teammates had not been in regular touch for years, he turned up for Marks' father's funeral. Something else to add to the mix of this supreme, generous and unforgettable cricketer.

Botham's form during the tour of New Zealand in 1978 cemented his place in the England team.

Botham was the highest profile member of the English team during his 15 years in the Test arena. Here he helps celebrate Australia's Bicentenary in 1988.

Len Hutton portrait from 1938.

Len Hutton with his wife Dorothy circa 1945.

*Hutton in 1947
at the Melbourne
Cricket Ground.*

Hutton ducks under a bumper from Lindwall during the fifth Test at The Oval, 1953.

Hobbs photographed in 1925, a particularly successful year for him, even by his lofty standards.

Wilfred Rhodes bowling in 1906.

Hammond meets King George VI mid-innings during the Second Test versus Australia at Lord's in 1938.

MCC touring party to Australia, 1928/29. Walter Hammond is second from left in the back row. Jack Hobbs is seated on the far right, front row.

HAMMOND, BOWLED TOSHACK   MILLER

DOOLAND

McCOOL

TALLON   HAMMOND

Hammond looks back at his stumps having been bowled by Ernie Toshack, Melbourne 1946/47. Wicketkeeper Tallon, and close fieldsmen McCool, Dooland and Miller applaud.

Wally Hammond straight drives Arthur Chipperfield on his way to a double-century in the second Test against Australia at Sydney in 1936/37.

James Anderson.

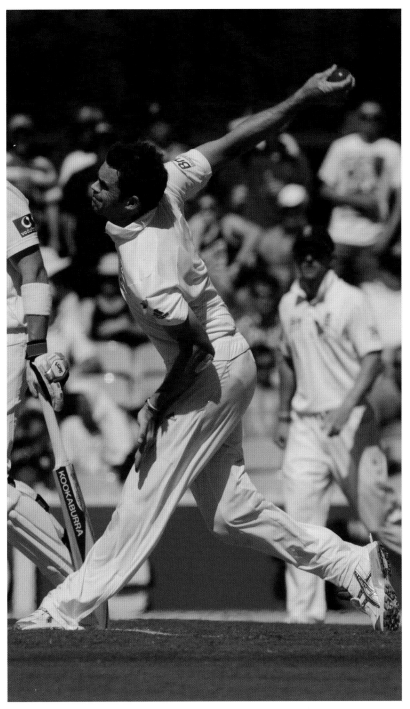

The purity of James Anderson's bowling action is the key to his longevity.

Ben Stokes is a true all-rounder, and one of the most powerful and explosive cricketers to play for England.

Stokes rose to prominence for England during the team's otherwise miserable 5-0 defeat to Australia in the Ashes of 2013/14.

Ian Botham

TESTS

Batting & Fielding

M	I	NO	Runs	HS	Ave	100	50	Ct	
102	161	6	5200	208	33.54	14	22	120	

Bowling

Balls	R	W	Ave	BBI	5	10	SR	Econ	
21815	10878	383	28.4	8–34	27	4	56.9	2.99	

ONE-DAY INTERNATIONALS

Batting & Fielding

M	I	NO	Runs	HS	Ave	SR	100	50	Ct
116	106	15	2113	79	23.21	79.10	0	9	36

Bowling

Balls	R	W	Ave	BBI	5	SR	Econ	
6271	4139	145	28.54	4–31	0	43.20	3.96	

FIRST-CLASS

Batting & Fielding

M	I	NO	Runs	HS	Ave	100	50	Ct	
402	617	4	19399	228	33.97	38	97	354	

Bowling

Balls	R	W	Ave	BBI	5	10	SR	Econ	
63547	31902	1172	27.22	8–34	59	8	54.52	3.01	

Alan Knott was named as one of the Wisden Cricketers of the Year in 1970.

8

ALAN KNOTT

Birth date	9 April 1946
Place of birth	Belvedere, Kent
Role	Wicketkeeper, right-handed middle-order batsman

"A thorough genius," was Mike Brearley's verdict; he is on record as rating Knott the greatest of all wicketkeepers.

In a sense wicketkeepers are cricket's true specialists. Each team has only one. He or she is intimately involved in every ball bowled while their side is in the field. They are likely to be involved in run-out possibilities: no one who saw it will forget Jos Buttler's glovework to run out Martin Guptill in the "Superover" that concluded the 2019 Men's World Cup. Caught behind is a statistically significant form of dismissal, stumped less so these days.

The keeper will stand back for the fast bowlers and stand up for the slow ones (the masters will sometimes stand up to medium-fast bowlers); two completely different skills.

Being a specialist means you don't do anything else. Obviously you don't bowl – though A. C. Smith famously took a hat-trick in a county match, and Australian Tim Zoehrer was a more than decent leg spinner. But in the old days you didn't have to bat either. Well, everybody bats – the keeper wasn't expected to make runs. Herbert Strudwick, who played in 28 Tests for England between 1909 and 1926, batted 42 times; in all but four of those innings he batted at 10 or 11 in the order. That would never happen now.

Alan Knott catches Paul Sheahan during the second Test at Lord's, 1968.
Colin Milburn is at short leg, Colin Cowdrey and Tom Graveney in the slips.

Knott puts everything into an appeal, 1970.

In Strudwick's day the wicketkeeper was supposed to be unobtrusive. That can still be regarded as a good thing. If you don't notice the keeper – and some of the more rarefied skills may go unnoticed – he or she has probably had a good day. But unobtrusiveness has gone out of fashion partly because chivvying is now a wicketkeeping KPI. Ian Healy's, "Bowled Warnie!" seemed as much a sound of the 90s as Blur or U2.

The England team that faced Australia in the fifth Test at The Oval in 1972. Back row, left to right: J H Hampshire, G G Arnold, A W Greig, D L Underwood, B Wood, A P E Knott. Front row, left to right: P H Parfitt, B L D'Oliveira, R Illingworth, J H Edrich, J A Snow.

How does Alan Knott rate when assessed using these parameters? Well, he certainly wasn't unobtrusive. His long-sleeved shirt always buttoned at the wrist, his collar always up, England cap – in the early part of his career – perched on a mass of dark hair, over piercing dark eyes.

Knott was an instantly recognisable cricketer. He was of average height, 5' 8", although he somehow seemed shorter, and very slim. His pointed jaw and angular features gave the impression of an almost elf-like figure behind the stumps; he had a ready grin and was an immensely popular player for both Kent and England. He used to do endless stretching exercises because he felt that he lacked natural suppleness. In fact, Knott was ahead of his time in terms of fitness and nutrition, his personal standards and requirements bordering on faddishness, in a manner not dissimilar to one of his successors, Jack Russell. He would shower and change his clothes at every interval, and appeared to subsist entirely on bananas and milk. He replaced his England cap with a floppy sun hat in the mid 1970s after injuring his neck in a car crash: the uplifted brim meant he could see more effectively without stretching his neck. He was paranoid about draughts arriving in even the warmest climates, wearing several layers of clothes.

Of his quality as a wicketkeeper there was no doubt. Oddly enough he had been a promising off spinner at school, but Les Ames, the Kent secretary-manager, and himself one of the greatest of all wicketkeeper-batsmen, saw him keeping in a Second XI match and knew at once that this was where his real talent lay.

Knott was incredibly nimble and agile, yet had the priceless capacity to concentrate for lengthy periods of time. He wasn't a showman, in the manner of another great Kent and England predecessor, Godfrey Evans. Nor was he what one of his captains, Brearley, called a "classical" wicketkeeper; he would occasionally take – or very occasionally drop – with one hand a chance that a more conventional gloveman might have attempted with two. And he defied the modern tendency, adopted with relish by Evans, to stand up to the medium-pacers. Knott said he stood back to reduce the risk of error. Of course he stood up for his great contemporary and Kent and England teammate "Deadly" Derek Underwood, whose unique brand of medium paced left-arm spin posed considerable challenges for batsmen and keepers alike. Knott and Underwood formed a strikingly successful partnership throughout the 1970s. During that period nobody had any doubt that Knott was the best wicketkeeper in the world.

The fact that Knott was a specialist keeper did not mean that his batting was of no consequence. On the contrary, he was a highly talented batsman, capable both of dogged and courageous defence and of inspired and often eccentric attack, the same nimble-footed perkiness that characterised his keeping being evident in his batting too. England often seemed to be in trouble with the bat in the 1970s, a bit like now. But Knott and the middle- or lower-middle order would often get them out of it. It might be with Basil D'Oliveira, or Tony Greig, or Ray Illingworth, or Peter Lever, but somehow it was always Knott. He made five Test centuries, two of them against Australia. There were plenty of good wicketkeepers around in those days, some outstanding ones, such as Bob Taylor but, as Brearley commented after Knott was preferred to Taylor midway through the 1981 Ashes series, it was Knott's batting that made the difference. Knott made 59 and 70 in the final two matches of that series, the last he played for England.

Knott made his Kent debut in 1964 and was firmly established as the first-choice keeper in 1965, making 84 dismissals. In 1966–67 he toured Pakistan with the MCC 'A' team under Brearley, and the following summer he made his Test debut, in the second Test against Pakistan at Trent Bridge. He claimed seven victims in that match, and six in the next at The Oval. This was enough to secure him a place on the tour of the West Indies that winter as reserve for Jim Parks.

Knott tries to stump Ian Chappell during the Third Test, at Edgbaston, 1968. Ken Barrington looks on imploringly from slip.

Parks was a brilliant batsman who turned himself into a wicketkeeper in the 1950s and was England's first-choice keeper for much of the 1960s. But his batting let him down in the Caribbean in 1967–68 and by the fourth Test, in Port of Spain, Knott was in the side. His inclusion had a decisive impact on the series, which England were to win one-nil.

The game at Port of Spain was the famous match where Gary Sobers declared setting England 214 in two and a half hours and England's captain Colin Cowdrey was reluctantly persuaded that England could win, which they did, by seven wickets (Geoff Boycott 80 not out, Cowdrey 71). But that victory would almost certainly not have been possible without Knott's 69 not out in England's first innings. Replying to West Indies' 526 for seven, England were struggling on 260 for five (having been 245 for two) when Knot joined Cowdrey. The Kent pair added 113, Knot batting, according to Wisden, "…with the aplomb of a veteran." Part-time leg spinner Basil Butcher then took four wickets in three overs and it was this, apparently, that convinced Sobers that England had a fatal weakness against wrist spin.

In the final Test, in Georgetown, Knott played an even more vital role. England had to bat through the sixth and final day to secure a draw, and the series. When Knott joined Cowdrey the score was 41 for five, of which Boycott had made 30. Again the Kent pair stood firm, adding 117. When Cowdrey was out for 82, Lance Gibbs' fifth wicket, seventy minutes remained. But Knott and the tail managed to survive, last man Jeff Jones playing out the final over. Knott made 73 not out in nearly four hours. Cowdrey described it as the longest day of his life. Knott selected his innings as the greatest of his life.

From then on Knott was a fixture in the England side until he joined Kerry Packer's World Series Cricket in 1977. During that period he played 89 of his 95 matches, including 65 in succession. He missed only one game between 1967–68 and 1977, the first Test against New Zealand at Christchurch in 1970–71, when perpetual understudy Taylor was given a game. In the following match, at Auckland, Knott made 101 and 96.

Knott is out for a duck in his first Test innings, against Pakistan at Trent Bridge in 1967. It is a double act for the Mohammed brothers, bowler Mushtaq and fielder Hanif. Wasim Bari is the wicketkeeper, Ken Barrington (who batted for nearly seven hours for 109 not out) the non-striker, and the umpire is Syd Buller.

That hundred was his first in Tests. He had narrowly missed a hundred in the series against Pakistan in 1968–69. This series was hastily arranged to replace the South African tour cancelled after the D'Oliveira crisis that erupted in the wake of England's victory over Australia at The Oval in the fifth Test of 1968. (England won the match thanks in part to a magnificent century from D'Oliveira. England bowled Australia out on a thrilling rain-affected final day, D'Oliveira made the vital breakthrough, bowling Barry Jarman with just 35 minutes to go; Underwood finished with seven wickets. There was a storm of outrage when, days later, the MCC party to tour South Africa was announced and D'Oliveira was not in it. Shortly after that the medium pacer Tom Cartwright withdrew from the tour party and D'Oliveira was selected in his place, whereupon the South African government, who ruled on the basis of race-based apartheid – D'Oliveira was a so-called "Cape Coloured" – cancelled the tour.) Knott had had a quiet series against Australia, although he made three stumpings in Australia's second innings at Headingley, all off off-spinner Illingworth, not something you see in many modern scorebooks. In Pakistan, the cricket was overshadowed by events off the field, the country being embroiled in political chaos. All the games were interrupted by riots and play was called off for good on the third day of the final Test in Karachi with Knott on 96 not out.

The Ashes contest that preceded that New Zealand series was one of a number of highlights of English cricket during this period. By this time Ray Illingworth had succeeded Cowdrey as captain and this tough, shrewd Yorkshireman built a highly competent side around him. His Ashes heroes were Boycott and the fast bowler John Snow but Knott was a key component. E. M. Wellings' Wisden tour report was clear on the point: "England's success was based primarily on Snow's bowling, the batting of Boycott, Edrich and Luckhurst, and the wicket-keeping of Knott." Knott claimed 21 catches and two stumpings in the Tests,

Wellings being especially impressed by his work standing back, where, he felt, his remarkable agility enabled him to take catches that others might not have recognised as chances.

The next Ashes encounter, in England in 1972, Illingworth's last in charge, saw Knott, if anything, in even more outstanding form, contributing much to a tight, competitive drawn series. He really came into his own in the fourth Test at Headingley when the teams were presented with a pitch affected by the fuserium virus, so that it took spin from the first day. The Australian batsmen had no answer to Underwood and Illingworth. Their captain, Ian Chappell, wrote years later, describing facing Underwood in these conditions: "These deliveries would turn and bounce making scoring for a right-hander difficult, and keeping wicket a nightmare, not that you'd ever have known from watching Alan Knott at work."

Chappell had cause to remember Knott from the final Test at The Oval too, which his side won to square the series. Knott top-scored with 92 in the first innings and made 63 in the second. Chappell described his eccentric method, "…facing up French-cricket style and then sweeping and cutting the spinners and driving the fast men crazy with his innovative strokeplay."

It was all very different when England next faced Australia, Down Under in 1974–75. The home side were armed with the fearsome pace of Dennis Lillee and the newly arrived Jeff Thomson. Mike Denness' England were beaten four-one. Knott was one of England's few successes. He and Greig were the only England players to appear in all six Tests, and between them made eight of England's 14 scores of over 50. Knott made a not-out century at the Adelaide Oval. In the course of the series, in which he effected 22 catches and one stumping, he overtook Evans to become the leading wicketkeeper in Test history.

He had claimed 16 victims in the three-match series against India the previous summer.

In 1976 England's batsmen were confronted by another fearsome pace attack, as Clive Lloyd led a young West Indian side still recovering from a mauling at the hands of Lillee and Thomson. Andy Roberts, Michael Holding and Wayne Daniel were ready to dish it out to new captain Greig's men. West Indies were, if not unstoppable, then unbeatable, winning the series three-nil. Greig and Knott were, with David Steele, the leading run-scorers. In the fourth Test at Headingley, when West Indies made an astonishing 437 for nine on the first day, Greig and Knott both made 116 in England's first innings, both starting with refreshing confidence but getting slower and slower. Knott spent over an hour in the 90s and batted for over five hours in all.

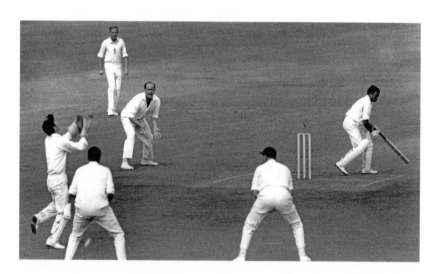

Alan Knott takes his first Test catch, in the second Test against Pakistan at Trent Bridge in 1967. The batsman is 'Billy' Ibadulla. Kent teammate Derek Underwood looks on from midwicket and captain Brian Close at short leg looks impressed. The slips are Basil D'Oliveira and Colin Cowdrey.

In 1976–77 he had a very successful tour of India, under Greig. He had first toured there in 1972–73 when Tony Lewis was captain and England had lost two-one to Ajit Wadekar's side, and Knott himself had an unusually underwhelming time. It was very different under Greig. The series was won three-one, and Knott made 268 runs at an average of 38 and dismissed 15 batsmen. Notwithstanding the margin of victory, England's main batsmen tended to proceed with extreme caution against India's fabled spinners, Eripalli Prasanna, Bhagwat Chandrasekhar and captain Bishan Singh Bedi. As Dicky Rutnagur put it in his tour review for Wisden, "[when] momentum was required, it was invariably provided by Knott, with his own brand of unorthodox batsmanship." He made a magnificent 75 in the first Test at New Delhi, which England unexpectedly won by an innings. Knott used his feet brilliantly against the spinners in what Rutnagur called an innings of "great impudence." He made 81 not out in the fourth Test at Bangalore, which India won.

Then came the celebrated Centenary Test at the MCG, which Australia won by 45 runs, as they had a century earlier. Knott made 42 in England's thrilling run chase.

And then Packer came calling, or rather his principal lieutenant, Greig. Knott was ready to listen. Nobody talked about burnout in those days but it is interesting to read Wisden's report on Knott's performance on the 1972–73 tour of India and Pakistan (they did them together in those days). This suggested that the reason for his lacklustre performance was "a surfeit of cricket". Since then he had toured the West Indies (1973–74), Australia and New Zealand (1974–75) and India. A real gripe of Knott's was the England cricket authorities' inflexibility with regard to families accompanying the players on tour. Whatever the reason, Knott was among the first players to sign up for the new "circus."

In the meantime, however, there was another Ashes series to play, his sixth. The English Packer players, including Greig, were picked for the 1977 series which the home side won three-nil. Knott averaged 36 and made his highest score in the third Test at Trent Bridge. This game, which England won by seven wickets, was noteworthy for the return to Test cricket, after a three year absence, of Boycott, who marked the occasion by running out the local hero Derek Randall. England were reduced to 82 for five in response to Australia's 243. Then Knott joined Boycott and the pair put on 215. Knott batted for two hours 50 minutes, Boycott (107) for six hours 18 minutes. Their stand remains the equal highest (with Len Hutton and Joe Hardstaff Jr at The Oval in 1938) for the sixth wicket against Australia, and Knott's innings remains the highest by an England wicketkeeper in an Ashes Test.

He was back in the England side – once the Australian cricket authorities had made peace with the television magnate Kerry Packer (changing the cricket landscape fundamentally and for all time) and Test cricket returned to normal – playing under Ian Botham against West Indies in 1980, and then for those last two Ashes Tests in 1981. He then opted to join the rebel tour of South Africa, which involved a three-year ban from international cricket. He was eligible for selection in the Ashes season of 1985 but, although there was no serious doubt that he was still the best keeper in the country, he wasn't picked. He retired from first-class cricket at the end of that season, aged 39.

Knott was surely one of England's greatest all-rounders, fit to rank with Botham. The final word should go to his first captain, Cowdrey: "I think he is the most gifted and dedicated cricketer one could ever wish to play with, never satisfied with his performance and always seeking for a little more perfection."

Alan Knott

TESTS

Batting & Fielding

M	I	NO	Runs	HS	Ave	100	50	Ct	St	
95	149	15	4389	135	32.75	5	30	250	19	

ONE-DAY INTERNATIONALS

Batting & Fielding

M	I	NO	Runs	HS	Ave	SR	100	50	Ct	St
20	14	4	200	50	20.00	80.97	0	1	15	1

FIRST-CLASS

Batting & Fielding

M	I	NO	Runs	HS	Ave	100	50	Ct	St	
511	745	134	18105	156	29.53	17	97	1211	133	

Bowling

Balls	R	W	Ave	BBI	5	10	SR	Econ	
104	87	2	43.5	1–5	0	0	52.00	5.01	

Wilfred Rhodes in his England touring blazer, 1908.

9

WILFRED RHODES

Birth date	29 November 1877; died 8 July 1973
Place of birth	Kirkheaton, Yorkshire
Role	Right-handed batsman, slow left-arm bowler

Wilfred Rhodes, according to Neville Cardus, was "Yorkshire cricket personified… And, in his spare time, so to say, he played for England."

In a first-class career that began in 1898 and ended in 1930, Rhodes took over 4,000 wickets and scored almost 40,000 runs. His Test record was not as sensational as that, but his Test career lasted almost as long as his first-class one. He played a pivotal role, in a number of guises, in some famous England victories. He played his first Test with W. G. Grace as captain. He and his fellow Yorkshireman, Emmot Robinson, were such favourites of Cardus (an adopted Lancastrian) – in Rhodes' case long after he retired as a player – that the writer created recognisable personalities to amuse his readers: he was, as it were, a Boswell to Rhodes' Johnson. According to Cardus' own biographer, Duncan Hamilton, Robinson once said to Cardus, "Tha' knows tha' made me oop?" Cardus denied it. "I enlarged him."

In his early years he was often associated with another great Yorkshire figure, George Hirst, like Rhodes a right-handed batsman and left-arm bowler, though Rhodes was an orthodox left-arm finger spinner while Hirst was a fast-medium swing bowler, who himself scored over 36,000 runs and took over 2700 wickets. Remarkably, both were born in Kirkheaton, a village three miles out of Huddersfield, though Rhodes was six years younger.

Hirst must certainly rank as one of the game's great all-rounders, though he didn't achieve the same level of success in Test cricket that Rhodes managed. They did, however, play the leading roles in one of the game's legendary stories.

The match was the fifth and final Test, at The Oval, of the great Ashes series of 1902. Australia dominated the game from the start, taking a first innings lead of 141. In their second innings, however, only Clem Hill reached 30, and England were set 263 to win. Australia's opening bowlers reduced them to 48 for five, but then Gilbert Jessop came in to play one of Test cricket's most remarkable innings. He reached his hundred (which included 17 fours and an all-run five – to get a six the ball had to be literally hit out of the ground) in 75 minutes, still the fastest by an England batsman in Tests. But when Jessop was out, 78 were still needed with only three wickets left. When Rhodes joined Hirst on the fall of the ninth wicket 15 were needed.

"We'll get 'em in singles," is the almost certainly apocryphal greeting given to Rhodes by Hirst (or possibly the other way round; nobody is quite sure). What is certain is that they didn't *get 'em in singles*. But they did get 'em. It shows what a good head Rhodes had on his shoulders; he was still only 24. It was a consolation win in a way – the Ashes were safely Australia's – but a tremendous game.

Rhodes bowling, 1923.

Rhodes in batting stance, 1926.

Rhodes and Hirst made an impact as a pair in the opening match of the series, at Edgbaston, when they bowled the Australians out for 36 (Rhodes seven for 17, Hirst three for 15), still Australia's lowest total against England. Rhodes opened the bowling in three of the five Tests (Australia did not bat in the rain-ruined match at Lord's) and was the leading England wicket-taker with 22 at 15.37. He batted throughout at 10 or 11, but headed the batting averages, being dismissed once while compiling 68 runs.

The wicket at Edgbaston was drying after heavy rainfall when Hirst and Rhodes set to work. In such conditions Rhodes could be unplayable. On perfect batting wickets he was extraordinarily difficult to get away. He claimed, surely with tongue in cheek, that he was never cut. Cardus told the story of Victor Trumper, one of Australia's greatest batsmen, and a darling of cricket's Golden Age, calling down to Rhodes during a Test in Melbourne, "For God's sake Wilfred, give me a minute's rest!"

He was a classical slow left-armer, genuinely slow, and apparently not a great spinner of the ball. For him, said Cardus, spin was "an accessory after the fact of flight." Relentless accuracy and control, small changes of pace and a delicious curving flight were the secrets of his success. A short and sturdy man, he could bowl immensely long spells. We can see pictures of him bowling, often in his cap in later years. There can be nobody living who can remember watching him bowl but Cardus provided a lovely description:

"The same familiar walk to the bowling crease, a few quick but easy steps, a little effortless leap, then the body comes through after a beautiful sidelong swing. No fuss, no waste...And so inscrutable!"

Remarkably, the Edgbaston Test of 1902 was only Rhodes' fourth. He had made an instant name for himself at Yorkshire, where he was the latest in a succession of great left-arm spinners that went on to include

Hedley Verity and Johnny Wardle. Rhodes' immediate predecessor, Bobby Peel, had his career abruptly terminated when he turned up for play one morning still suffering from the effects of the night before, marked out his run, and bowled an immaculate delivery in the direction of the sightscreen. Rhodes was of a very different ilk.

In 1899 he took 179 first-class wickets at 17 apiece and played in the last three Ashes Tests. In 1900 and 1901 he took 261 and 251 wickets respectively. Yorkshire refused to allow him or Hirst to tour Australia with the MCC side in 1901–02, so 1902 was his next chance of international cricket. From then on, he was a regular until after the First World War.

Plum Warner's MCC side regained the Ashes in 1903–04, winning the first two Tests and the fourth. Rhodes' impact on the first two games was critical. The first Test, at Sydney, which England won by five wickets, was notable for R. E. Foster's 287, still the highest score by an England batsman in a Test in Australia. He and Rhodes (40) put on 130 for the tenth wicket, still England's highest against Australia, and their highest against anyone until Joe Root and James Anderson put on 198 against India in 2014.

In Australia's second innings of that match the hosts piled up 485, with Trumper carrying his bat for 185. Rhodes' figures in that innings were 40.2 overs, 10 maidens, five for 94. Cardus called it one of the greatest bowling performances of all time. There was no spin; he got his wickets through, "subtlety in the air."

In the second Test at Melbourne, England won a critical toss and, batting first, made 315, having at one point been 277 for two. In Australia's first innings, only the magnificent Trumper could cope with the conditions; he made 74 out of 122. Rhodes, who opened the bowling with Hirst, took seven for 56, including four of the top five.

In their second innings, England made 103. J. T. Tyldesley, who had scored 97 in the first innings, scored 62; the next highest score was 10. Australia were then bowled out for 111, Rhodes taking eight for 68. He bowled unchanged throughout the match, and had match figures of 15 for 124. Only Jim Laker and Hedley Verity have taken more wickets for England in a Test against Australia.

In the series as a whole Rhodes took 31 wickets at 15.74 apiece. No slow bowler has taken more wickets in a series for England in Australia. Warwick Armstrong really suffered during the series. Armstrong, nicknamed the Big Ship, a leading all-rounder and future Australian captain, was dismissed eight times out of 10 by Rhodes in the series.

At this point, in the first half of the first decade of the new century, Rhodes must have been at the height of his powers as a slow left-arm bowler. Yet it was around this time that he began the process of converting himself into a different player, thus earning the right to be recognised as one of the most extraordinary of all all-round cricketers.

He was always useful as a batsman but now he moved up the order often appearing at number seven or eight after having previously batted at every position for England. As one would expect with so shrewd an operator, this was at least partly a matter of self-preservation. He wasn't the only slow left-armer in town. England would often pick Colin Blythe, of Kent, as well as Rhodes, and his county colleague, Frank Woolley, developing into a great all-rounder.

Rhodes moved up the order to number three in the final Test of the Ashes series of 1909, making 66 and 54, and then opened the batting with considerable success in the series against South Africa in 1909–10. Thus it was that when MCC toured Australia under J. W. H. T. Douglas in 1911–12, Rhodes opened the batting with Jack Hobbs.

Wilfred Rhodes driving into the covers in 1904.

This Ashes series, which England won four-one after losing the first Test, has always been regarded as one of English cricket's greatest triumphs. There were a number of reasons for this, including the bowling of S. F. Barnes and Frank Foster, but the batting partnership of Hobbs and Rhodes was central to that success.

In the first three Tests, their partnerships were 45 (Hobbs went on to make 63), and 29, 10 (Rhodes 61) and 57 (Hobbs 126 not out, in a successful chase of 219 for two) and 147 (Hobbs 187, Rhodes 59) and five (Rhodes 57 not out in a successful chase of 112 for two.)

And then, in the fourth Test, at the MCG, after Australia had made 191, Hobbs and Rhodes put on an opening stand of 323 in 268 minutes. This remains England's record opening partnership against Australia.

Hobbs was first out, for 178; Rhodes then added 112 with George Gunn, finishing on 179, made in just under seven hours.

In the fifth Test, which Australia won, they put on 16 and 76.

And Rhodes' bowling on this triumphant tour? He bowled not a single ball in the Tests.

And so things continued, for a little while. He was a consistent performer in the Triangular Trophy in 1912 (involving Australia and South Africa, and incorporating a three-match Ashes series, which England won) putting on two century stands with Hobbs in the games against Australia at Lord's and The Oval. He had a fine tour of South Africa in 1913–14, making 152 in the innings victory in Johannesburg.

Unlike his classically refined bowling action, Rhodes' batting was, by all accounts, not a thing of beauty. It was just wonderfully effective. From an aesthetic point of view he must have suffered in comparison with Hobbs, whom he partnered in most of his big Test innings. Hobbs was a genuine artist with the bat, and he himself always maintained that he was a better player before the First World War. Rhodes was a plodder by comparison. He was also one of the first batsmen to adopt a two-eyed stance. (Cricket is essentially a side-on game, for batsmen and bowlers. Some batsmen turn their bodies in the stance so that they are much more front-on, almost like French cricket; the West Indian Shivnarine Chanderpaul is an example, the English all-rounder Peter Willey another.) Rhodes was a pioneer of this style. He was extremely difficult to get out. One thing Hobbs and Rhodes had in common was that they were both brilliant runners between the wickets. Among England's opening pairs, in terms of average runs per partnership, Hobbs and Rhodes (61) come second to Hobbs and Herbert Sutcliffe (87).

By the time the War was over Rhodes had turned 40. Yorkshire had lost two leading spinners in the conflict, Abe Waddington and Major

Booth, and when county cricket resumed, they asked him if he would mind picking up his bowling again. Not a problem at all. In 1919 he took the little matter of 164 wickets at 14 apiece, as well as making over 1200 runs. In 1920 it was 161 wickets at 13 apiece.

Then came the first international challenge since the War – the tour of Australia in 1920–21. This turned out to be a terrible mismatch, with Australia's bowling, led by fast bowler Jack Gregory and leg-spinner Arthur Mailey, overpowering the Englishmen. Rhodes had a middling series, though he did become the first player to score 2,000 runs and take 100 wickets in Tests. (Only two England players have scored a thousand runs and taken a hundred wickets in Ashes Tests: Rhodes and Ian Botham.)

The teams then went back to England on the same boat to resume hostilities in the summer of 1921. Armstrong's men won the first three Tests easily, England having no answer to the pace of Jack Gregory and Ted MacDonald; Rhodes was dropped after the first. (England used 30 players in the series, 17 of whom played in only one Test.) That, surely, was the end.

But no, in 1926 Rhodes scored 1,100 runs at an average of 34 and took 115 wickets at an average of 14, heading the national bowling averages. This was the sixteenth and last time he achieved the double of a thousand runs and a hundred wickets in a first-class season. Nobody else did it more than 14 times (that was Hirst). He was now 48.

It was another Ashes summer. England had now lost three series in a row. But there were signs that things were changing. They had actually won the final Test of the 1924–25 campaign. Uniquely in an Ashes series, the first four Tests were drawn.

The England selectors – to whose number Hobbs and Rhodes had been co-opted – took some bold decisions for the fifth Test at

The Oval. The captain, Arthur Carr, was replaced by the young Percy Chapman. And there were two bowlers yet to appear in the series: debutant pace bowler Harold Larwood, and Rhodes himself. The Oval, 1926, was a classic Test match. It was a "timeless" Test, played to a finish. England made 280 (Sutcliffe 76, Mailey 6 for 138). Australia responded with 302. Rhodes took 2 for 35 in 25 overs, including the critical wicket of opener Bill Woodfull, bowled for 35. Hobbs and Sutcliffe had an awkward hour and a bit to get through at the end of the second day. In the event they responded with perhaps their greatest opening stand, despite overnight rain making conditions very difficult for batting. They added 172 (Hobbs 100, Sutcliffe 161), England making 436. Australia were overwhelmed on the fourth day, bowled out for 125. The first seven in the order fell to Larwood and Rhodes. Rhodes took four for 44 in 20 overs. And England held The Ashes for the first time since 1912.

Amazingly, his Test career was not over. In 1929–30 MCC took the unprecedented – and not repeated – step of sending two tour parties overseas, one to New Zealand and one to the West Indies. Rhodes was in the West Indies party and played all four Tests; the series was drawn one-all. He batted at number 10, and bowled huge numbers of overs, 78 in the drawn first Test at Bridgetown. In the final Test at Kingston his match figures were 44.5 overs, 25 maidens, two for 39. It was also Rhodes' last Test: his international career had spanned an astonishing 31 years.

He retired at the end of the 1930 season, having appeared once against Don Bradman. "Right good player," he told Jack Fingleton in 1953; there was no higher praise from Rhodes. He took a wicket with his final ball in first-class cricket.

Batting, bowling and fielding (Rhodes took 764 catches in first-class cricket, seventh on the all-time list) were not the whole story. Rhodes had a vast store of cricketing knowledge and was expert at deploying it and at passing it down. It was a hard school, the Rhodes-Robinson academy in Yorkshire. There is a story of a young bowler returning to the dressing room with figures of seven for 26, expecting congratulations; instead, he got a reprimand – it should have been seven for 22. In the old days of the amateur/professional divide, most county captains were nice but dim, or at least dim. Nobody doubted that Rhodes was the de facto captain of Yorkshire in the 1920s. After The Oval Test in 1926, Chapman was the most popular man in England. That was because, Rhodes used to say, he had the common sense to do what Jack Hobbs and I told him.

He did indeed typify a certain type of "…cautious, taciturn, detached" Yorkshireman, as Simon Wilde has put it. Rhodes, according to Hamilton, "was never discreet with his criticism. If he didn't like a player, he told him so. If he didn't rate him either, considering him a liability, his backside wouldn't touch a bench in the dressing room." In later years, particularly after being afflicted with blindness, he seemed to become warmer and more voluble. That is the impression gained from reading accounts of conversations with him by writers such as Cardus and Fingleton. Cardus wrote an essay about a conversation with Rhodes in 1950. One of the many things he talked about was his 179 at Melbourne in 1911–12. "Ah borrowed George [Gunn]'s bat, and d'yo' know, when Ah starts playing forward, just defensive, ball goes for four, ay, just defensive push and it goes for four, aye, it goes for four, just a defensive push…" His face, according to Cardus, "suffused with joy – nearly half a century after the event." He continued to watch or listen to cricket to the very end.

Cardus last saw him, a few weeks before his death in 1973 at the grand old age of 95, leaving Trent Bridge after a day at the Test, arm in arm with his daughter and son-in-law, "His face ruddy after hours sitting and listening to cricket and whether he knew it or not, himself a permanent part of the game's history and tradition."

Wilfred Rhodes

TESTS

Batting & Fielding

M	I	NO	Runs	HS	Ave	100	50	Ct
58	98	21	2325	179	30.19	2	11	60

Bowling

Balls	R	W	Ave	BBI	5	10	SR	Econ
8231	3245	127	26.96	8-68	6	1	64.81	

FIRST-CLASS

Batting & Fielding

M	I	NO	Runs	HS	Ave	100	50	Ct
1107	1528	237	39802	267*	30.83	58	196	764

Bowling

Balls	R	W	Ave	BBI	5	10	Rate	
184142	69993	4187	16.71	9-24	287	68	43.97	

In 1966 Fred Trueman was 35 years old but still menacing.

10

FRED TRUEMAN

Birth date	6 February 1931, died 1 July 2006
Place of birth	Scotch Springs, Maltby, Yorkshire
Role	Right-arm fast bowler

*"T' Definitive Volume of t' Finest Bloody Fast Bowler that
Ever Drew Breath."*

This was the disarmingly modest suggestion by Fred Trueman for the title of the biography of him written by John Arlott (and called simply "Fred"). It is worth examining how Trueman's assessment of his own capabilities, undoubtedly heartfelt, stands up to serious examination.

He was, famously, the first man to reach 300 Test wickets: he reached the landmark during the fifth Test against Australia at The Oval in 1964. He had been the world's leading Test wicket-taker since the New Zealand series in 1962–63, relieving teammate Brian Statham of that mantle: it was his until 1976 when the West Indian off-spinner Lance Gibbs overtook him.

A classic fast bowler's action and a look of real menace; Fred Trueman during the third Test against India in 1952.

Since then an additional 31 bowlers have taken at least 300 Test wickets. Many of course have gone well beyond that. Trueman reached the landmark in his 65th Test. Only nine other bowlers have done it faster, in terms of matches played. Only six of those are pace bowlers, and they are the very best: Dennis Lillee (56), Malcolm Marshall, Richard

Hadlee and Dale Steyn (61), Allan Donald (63) and Glenn McGrath (64). Among England bowlers, Ian Botham reached 300 wickets in 72 Tests, Bob Willis and James Anderson in 81.

Trueman had a strike rate of 49.4 in Tests. Of pace bowlers with at least 300 Test wickets, only Steyn (42.3), Waqar Younis (43.4), Marshall (46.7) and Donald (47) have done better.

For most students of the game, it is the career average that is the truest indicator of quality. Trueman played only 67 Tests but they were spread over 13 years. He had a remarkable career average of 21.57. As at the time of writing – October, 2019 – that puts him at 30th in the all-time list of bowlers who have delivered at least 2,000 balls in Test cricket. Of that list, 10 of the top 12 played predominantly before World War One. Of what one might call Trueman's peer group – fast bowlers with at least 300 Test wickets – there are only two with better averages: Marshall (20.94) and Curtly Ambrose (20.99). (His high-speed contemporary, Frank Tyson, had a career average of 18.56 and a strike rate of 15.4 but took only 76 wickets in 17 Tests.)

These numbers put Trueman at the very top of the fast bowling tree. As a presence on and off the field, he was utterly memorable. He was of medium height, with craggy features and a mop of black hair. Built to be a fast bowler, broad-shouldered, deep-chested and with immensely strong legs, Trueman had a beautiful classical action. A rhythmically accelerating and smooth run-up led to a perfect side-on action with an almost exaggerated delivery stride. Arlott described his action at the point of delivery: "He was a cocked trigger, left arm pointed high, head steady, his eyes glaring at the batsman as that great stride widened, the arm slashed down and as the ball was fired down the pitch, his body was thrown hungrily after it, the right toe raking the ground closely beside the wicket as he swept on."

This action made him a master of the outswinger, his most potent weapon throughout his long career. At his best he swung it late and at high pace, and he could be a nightmare to face. For variety, he would bowl wide of the crease, and bring the ball into the right-handers; once he had mastered the yorker, this became another formidable weapon.

At the beginning of his career Trueman was an out-and-out paceman, genuinely fast, with an irresistible fondness for the bouncer. Control was often a problem in his early years but when everything worked he could be irresistible.

Later in his career, when he was in what Arlott called his "pomp", he would sometimes reduce his pace and bowl off-cutters. It was in this role that he produced one of his most memorable Test performances, bowling England to victory against Richie Benaud's Australians at Headingley in 1961. By then he was the complete package, a thinking bowler who could work out how he was going to dismiss the best batsmen. He made a close study of the Australian Ray Lindwall, the world's best fast bowler in the years after World War Two.

And he always had the fast bowler's mentality. He was an aggressive cricketer in everything he did, whether bowling, batting (a good enough player to make two first-class hundreds) or fielding – he was, unusually for a fast bowler, a brilliant short leg fielder and a terrific catcher. He was always "after" batsmen. One of his legendary tactics, especially in county cricket for his beloved Yorkshire, was to go into the opposition dressing room and greet their batsmen and tell them how he was going to get them out. In some ways the "modern" player who most reminds one of Trueman is Shane Warne. Both of them were supremely confident on the field, to the point of arrogance, and each had a very good "cricket brain". For each of them, especially in the latter part of their respective careers, psyching the batsman out was half the battle.

A day at the races: MCC tour manager the Duke of Norfolk, captain Ted Dexter, John Murray and Fred Trueman at the Melbourne Cup, November 1962.

Off the field Trueman was more complicated than his on-field bluster would indicate. As he got older there was plenty of off-field bluster too; by the time he finished as part of a memorable Test Match Special team he had almost become a caricature of himself, with his celebrated catchphrase "I don't know what's goin' off out there." In his younger days, despite the apparent self-confidence there was an underlying insecurity. This could lead to awkward moments. He had a difficult time on Len Hutton's tour of the Caribbean in 1953–54. His tour bonus was withheld on the basis of a report from Hutton that he had been an embarrassment. Trueman's autobiography relates a few incidents – arguments with umpires, some alleged late night cavorting (he said the principal culprit was Godfrey Evans.) Not surprisingly he pleads innocent. He deeply resented being singled out; he said the tour was marked by ill-will between the teams, and discord within the England camp, many of the senior players thinking Hutton's approach was too negative. When the players got home Trueman asked Hutton why he had been fined but never got a satisfactory answer. As a result of this he was omitted from the party that toured Australia successfully under Hutton the following winter. He was to tour Australia twice. He made it clear in his memoirs that he did not enjoy the second tour, under Ted Dexter, in 1962–63. This came straight after the abolition of the distinction in cricket between amateurs and professionals. It was hardly the dawn of a new era. The manager, astonishing as it may seem, was the Duke of Norfolk. The opening batsman was the Rev. David Sheppard. At a press conference early on in the tour, Trueman said he was "a bit confused, in that I didn't know whether we were supposed to be playing under Jockey Club rules [His Grace was the President], for Dexter Enterprises, or engaged on a missionary hunt."

Trueman liked Dexter, but had limited respect for him as a captain, "More theories than Charles Darwin." Special irritation was reserved for Sheppard, the future bishop of Liverpool, opening batsman, and frustratingly inconsistent slip fielder.

"Pretend it's Sunday, Reverend, and keep your hands together."

He never had much time for Oxbridge types.

Trueman was born (weighing in at 14lb 1oz) and grew up in a mining community in South Yorkshire. His father was a coal miner and Trueman worked down the pit himself until cricket and National Service took him out. He made an early impact at Yorkshire and made his debut for England in 1952 in the first Test against India at Headingley.

He had a quiet first innings, taking three for 89, but in the second, before a crowd of more than 30,000, his sheer pace reduced India to nought for four; England won by seven wickets. "Here at last," as Arlott said, "was an English fast bowler who by a spectacular performance had turned a Test match." He took four wickets in each innings of the second Test at Lord's, which England won by eight wickets. Then, at Old Trafford, where England won by an innings, he took eight for 31, still England's best innings figures against India. The Indian opener Pankaj Roy bagged a pair: in all he made five ducks in the four-match series. Trueman took five wickets in India's only innings in the drawn final Test at The Oval. He took 29 wickets in the series at 13.31, still the record for an England bowler in a series against India.

That didn't make him an England regular, not yet. 1953 was an Ashes year. Trueman was still doing his National Service and could not play cricket as and when he wanted. But everyone was talking about him. Jack Fingleton left the tourists' game against the Minor Counties at Stoke to watch the Roses match at Old Trafford in the hope of seeing Trueman.

He was impressed by the run-up – "...from here to eternity..." – but not so much by the pace. Fingleton thought the length of the run-up made Trueman seem faster than he was. "He *looks* fast."

The series was poised nil-all as England's selectors met to pick the team for the final Test at The Oval. For the first time in the series Hutton was persuaded to go with four specialist bowlers; and Trueman was one of them. He played a worthy part in a famous victory, taking four wickets in Australia's first innings.

Now Fingleton was impressed, "Erratic, yes: wild, most certainly; but full of fire and dynamic."

Trueman demonstrating his grip, 1962.

That got him on the plane to the Caribbean in 1953–54, where almost everything went wrong for him. He played in three Tests and took nine wickets at an average of 46, but that was the least of his problems. Arlott thought Hutton understood him as a bowler but not as a man. Whatever the cause, Trueman was banished to the fringes of the England side, missing not only the Ashes tour of 1954–55 (the triumph of Tyson and Statham) but also Peter May's tour of South Africa in 1956–57. So by the start of the series against West Indies in 1957, he had played only 11 Tests, four of them in that series against India.

And then, all of a sudden, everything came together for him. In the next four home summers, England won series against West Indies, New Zealand, India and South Africa; they also beat West Indies away in 1959–60. These victories owed much to the exceptional bowling partnership between Trueman and the Lancastrian, Statham, who took a combined 284 wickets in the 35 Tests they played together. They took 41 wickets in the five Tests against India in 1959 and 52 against South Africa in 1960. Apart from being superb right-arm fast bowlers from the north of England, they had absolutely nothing in common.

The only blip was Australia in 1958–59, when an apparently strong England side, including Trueman, Statham and Tyson, was overwhelmed by Australia's draggers and chuckers – in particular Ian Meckiff and Gordon Rorke – and, to be fair, Benaud and the supremely gifted Alan Davidson. Australia won a close-fought and intriguing series in 1961, when Trueman had perhaps his single greatest match.

The Ashes tour of 1962–63, a dullish draw, was the great duo's last hurrah together: Trueman took 20 wickets at 26. Statham was beginning to struggle and took 13 wickets at 44. On the New Zealand leg of the tour Trueman took 14 wickets in two Tests at an average of 11.71. Then in 1963, against an immensely powerful West Indies side, when Statham was dropped after the first Test, and Trueman was thought to be past his best, he took an extraordinary 34 wickets in the series at an average of 17.47, still the record for the number of wickets taken by an England bowler in a series against West Indies.

The tour of the West Indies in 1959–60 was the first time Trueman showed he could be a decisive figure overseas. This was a high-scoring series, dominated by the batsmen. Gary Sobers, emerging gradually as one of the world's greatest players, scored 703 runs at an average of 101 in the five-match series. There were four draws. England won the second Test at Port of Spain by 256 runs.

Sobers, caught Barrington b Trueman 0, in the first innings, lbw b Trueman 31, in the second.

In the series, Trueman took 21 wickets at an average of 20. England won the series one-nil.

Australia were one up when the teams went to Headingley for the third Test of the 1961 Ashes series. The visitors made a steady start on the first day, and although the pitch showed early signs of unpredictable behaviour, Norman O'Neill and Neil Harvey looked untroubled as they batted through the afternoon session. The new ball was taken with the score on 183 for two. Before long they were 208 for nine, and were all out for 237; Trueman took five wickets for 16 runs in six overs.

In retrospect this was the spell that won the match for England, but things actually got better for Trueman. England's lead was restricted to 62 and when Australia batted a second time, Harvey again looked in control. Trueman was brought on with the score on 98 for three. He shortened his run-up and bowled off-cutters. This time he took five wickets for no runs in 16 balls, the score lurched to 109 for eight and 120 all out. Trueman had match figures of eleven for 88 and, as Benaud said, became a hero overnight. Benaud himself, who was returning from injury after missing Australia's victory at Lord's, bagged a pair, twice clean bowled by Trueman.

Trueman gets Manjrekar LBW for 17 during the first Test versus India, 1959.

(In the fourth Test at Old Trafford, Benaud bowled his side to a famous series-clinching victory. Trueman got the blame for creating the footholes into which Benaud pitched his legbreaks, and was dropped for the fifth Test at The Oval.)

Trueman (centre) looks up as Brian Close raises the Gilette Cup, 1965. Doug Padgett, John Hampshire, Ken Taylor (partly obscured), Ray Illingworth and Jimmy Binks are also in the group.

Frank Worrell brought an immensely strong side to England in 1963, winning the series three-one. In the two games England didn't lose – the sensational draw at Lord's in the second Test, and their comprehensive win at Edgbaston in the third – Trueman was a dominant figure.

It is worth spending some time on the Lord's game.

It is an odd thing that the 1960s, which in general was Test cricket's most boring decade, should have produced two of the few Test matches to have inspired a book all to itself. The first was the Brisbane tied Test which has inspired more than one.

The second was Lord's, 1963. Just as Brisbane 1960-61 has its iconic image – West Indies' fielders exulting as Joe Solomon's side-on throw hit the stumps to run out Ian Mackiff – so Lord's 1963 has the strangely downbeat but instantly evocative snapshot: Colin Cowdrey emerging from the Pavilion with his arm in plaster – broken by a ball from Wes Hall when England were 72 for three in the second innings. Two balls to be played and England needing six runs to win, with one wicket left. Of course Cowdrey did not have to face a ball – the ninth wicket pair David Allan and Derek Shackleton had crossed so it was Allen who played out the last two balls for a draw, but that is really not the point.

West Indies had won the first Test at Old Trafford easily, Conrad Hunte making a big hundred and Lance Gibbs taking 11 wickets. At Lord's, the two sides were level after one innings, West Indies making 301 (Trueman, six for 100) and England 297: Dexter's 70 was one of Test cricket's most genuinely memorable innings, "Lord Ted" standing tall and driving and hooking Hall and Charlie Griffith.

West Indies went in again on the third afternoon and were soon in trouble, and when Worrell came in to join Basil Butcher the score was 104 for five and England were very much on top. But Butcher played the innings of his life, one that in the context of the match was comparable with Dexter's. He made 133 in nearly four and a half hours adding 110 with Worrell (33).

West Indies were 214 for five at the close on Saturday but lost their last five wickets in a rush on Monday morning, Trueman finishing with five for 52. England needed 234 to win. Micky Stewart, John Edrich and Dexter were out with only 31 on the board. Ken Barrington and Cowdrey played well against fearsomely fast bowling but then Cowdrey, retired hurt. When play was abandoned for bad light at 4.45pm, England were 116 for three.

Rain delayed play until 2.30pm on the last day, putting exquisite strain on the age-old equation of runs, wickets and time. Barrington continued to exude defiance adding 60 to his first innings (80) but the lead role was assumed by Brian Close who in an innings that excited considerable controversy, took the attack, at considerable physical risk, to Hall and Griffith. He was eventually out, charging down the wicket to Hall, for 70.

When Shackleton joined Allen, 19 were required in 15 minutes. In the age of T20 it is hard not to regard the denouement as somewhat anti-climactic. Worrell entrusted last over, as he did at Brisbane, to the magnificent Hall ("Don't bowl a no-ball"). The 38-year-old Shackleton was not out off the good ball. Allen played out those last two balls. Nobody could say a draw was not a fair result.

Trueman took six wickets in West Indies' first innings and five in the second. His figures on the first day were five for 64 in 32 overs, demonstrating, in Alan Ross's words, that "In fast bowling, as in lovemaking, control brings greater rewards than youthful impetuosity." At Edgbaston he took five for 75 and a dramatic seven for 44, as West Indies were bowled out for 131. He took the last six wickets in 24 deliveries; Arlott called it, "Cold, objective, knowledgeable killing."

The 1964 Ashes was not one of the great series. It is remembered for two things, both involving Trueman. The only Test to reach a positive result was the third, at Headingley, which Australia won by seven wickets. The crucial passage of play came on the second afternoon when, with Australia on 187 for seven (England having made 268 in their first innings) Dexter took the new ball. Commentators often muse that taking the new ball can backfire: this is the textbook illustration. Trueman kept pitching short; Peter Burge, who made 160, the innings of his life, kept hitting him to the boundary. Australia made 389 (Trueman three for 98 in 24 overs), an unusually high strike rate for those generally more pedestrian days.

He was dropped for the fourth Test which was just as well (Australia 656 for 8, and four for none; England 611). The two sides literally ground each other into the dust over five inexorable days. He was back for the fifth at The Oval. He took four wickets in Australia's only innings, all coming before lunch on the third day, with two off successive balls, both caught at slip by Colin Cowdrey; the second of these, Neil Hawke, was Trueman's 300th in Tests.

That would have been a good time to call it a day. He lingered on for a bit more, long enough to express disgruntlement at being excluded from Mike Smith's tour of South Africa, and to play a couple of Tests against New Zealand in 1965.

He remained a force in county cricket. He was a shrewd stand-in captain, leading Yorkshire to a famous win over Bill Lawry's Australians in 1968, his final year. Yorkshire won six championship titles between 1959 and 1968. No fast bowler has approached his total of 2,304 first-class wickets at 18.29. In the late 1950s and early 1960s he regularly bowled over a thousand overs a season.

And as he got older, and became more skilful, he never lost that self-belief that had marked him out as a colt. Arlott tells a great story from the last years. Yorkshire had beaten Leicestershire, and Trueman was regaling his teammates with a description of how he had done it. Richard Hutton was suitably impressed, "You must have bowled the lot, Fred – inners, outers, yorkers, slower ones – but tell me – did you ever bowl a plain straight ball?" There was no pause from Fred: "Aye, I did – to Peter Marner and it went straight through him like a stream of piss and flattened all three."

Fred Trueman

TESTS

Batting & Fielding

M	I	NO	Runs	HS	Ave	100	50	6s	Ct	St
67	85	14	981	39*	13.81	0	0	25	64	0

Bowling

Balls	R	W	BBI	BBI	Ave	Econ	SR	4w	5w	10
15178	6625	307	8–31	12–119	21.57	2.61	49.40	19	17	3

FIRST-CLASS

Batting & Fielding

M	I	NO	Runs	HS	Ave	100	50	6s	Ct	St
603	713	120	9231	104	15.56	3	26	25	439	0

Bowling

Balls	R	W	BBI	BBM	Ave	Econ	SR	4w	5w	10
99701	42154	2304.00	8–28		18.29	2.53	43.2		126	25

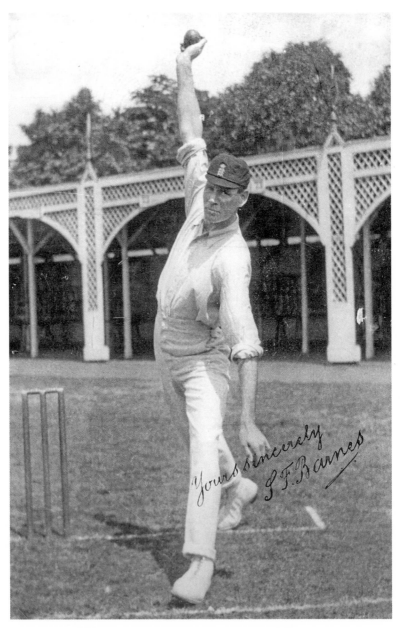

Barnes posing on the Nursery Ground at Lord's, 1901.

11

SYDNEY BARNES

Birth date	19 April 1873, died 26 December 1967
Place of birth	Smethwick, Staffordshire
Role	Right-arm medium-pace bowler

"Right-arm medium-pace bowler" does not quite do justice to S. F. Barnes. It seems an accurate description of Darren Stevens, say, or Ken MacKay, but S. F. Barnes? Isn't he supposed to be one of the greatest bowlers of all time?

What sort of bowler was Barnes then? He often opened the bowling in Tests, so he must surely have been quite fast. He did indeed start as an outright fast bowler but soon realised, as Jack Fingleton put it, "That there was more to the business than sheer speed." He would vary his pace to suit conditions but, essentially, according to the cricket historian H. S. Altham, he bowled at "… appreciably more than medium pace." In the 1911-12 Ashes series, he opened the bowling with the left-armer Frank Foster, who was definitely fast-medium. But, like the great medium-fast bowler of the 1920s, Maurice Tate, Barnes could generate pace off the pitch. Clem Hill, the fine left-hander who captained Australia in that series, told Neville Cardus about the challenges of facing Barnes on the celebrated day in Melbourne when he took five for one, "Some of us carried blue and yellow bruises on our thighs for days. He made them come faster from the pitch than Foster did and Foster was faster through the air."

Barnes demonstrating his grip, 1902.

Was he a swing bowler or a spin bowler? Remarkably, he seems to have been both. Fingleton described him thus: "When Barnes swung in the air from the leg, by spin, the ball turned back from the off. When he swung in from the off, with his leg break action, the ball gripped the pitch with spin and turned from the leg." Hill, who made successive scores of 99, 98 and 97 for Australia against England in 1911–12, told Cardus that on a perfect wicket Barnes could swing the ball in and out very late and "spin from the ground, pitch outside the leg stump and miss the off." As his record at home and away amply demonstrates, he could adapt his method to suit any type of surface.

Altham gave a graphic description of his action and his variations. "A run, not long but full of life and spring, a high delivery, and the head leading a full and perfectly balanced follow-through – that was the basic machinery that commanded such control of length and direction; but the secret of his mastery lay in the supple steel of his fingers and hand... [H]e could, even in the finest weather and on the truest wickets in Australia, both swing and break the ball from off and leg. Most deadly of all was the ball which he would deliver from rather wide on the crease, move in with a late swerve the width of the wicket, and then straighten back off the ground to hit the off stump."

This was the so-called *Barnes' Ball*. When he bowled the immortal Victor Trumper for a duck at Melbourne in 1907–08, Charlie Macartney was standing at the bowler's end. He told Fingleton about the dismissal, "The ball was fast on the leg stump, but just before it pitched it swung suddenly to the off. Then it pitched, broke back, and took Vic's leg stump. It was the sort of ball a man might see if he was dreaming or drunk."

In the 1930s – long after Barnes had left the international scene, cricket people would debate whether he or Bill O'Reilly, the great

Australian leg-spinner, who also operated at medium pace, were the better bowler. Don Bradman observed that O'Reilly had all Barnes' tricks – and one that he didn't have: Barnes didn't bowl the googly (the leg-spinner's "wrong'un" that turns from off to leg). Cardus put this argument to Barnes, who replied, with eyes glinting, "It's quite true. I didn't bowl the googly. I never needed it."

Barnes during the tour of South Africa, 1913.

Then there was his attitude, his demeanour. It wasn't that he was overtly aggressive, like a fast bowler in the manner of Dennis Lillee, say. But a batsman had no doubt what Barnes felt about him. "Very daunting and very relentless," said John Woodcock. "Why do these bowlers today send down so many balls the batsmen don't need to play?" he asked Cardus while watching a Test. "I didn't ever give 'em any rest."

And as Cardus put it "…a chill wind of antagonism blew from him even on the sunniest day." This unique and extraordinary bowler took 189 wickets in 27 Tests. He took his last 100 Test wickets in just 11 matches. He took his 100th wicket in his 17th Test, and was the first man to take 150 wickets in Tests, reaching the landmark in his 24th Test; Waqar Younis and Yasir Shah are the next fastest, each taking 27 matches. He took 34 wickets in England's famous series victory in Australia in 1911–12. The following English summer, 1912, he took 34 wickets in the three Tests against South Africa in the Triangular Tournament. Then in 1913–14, in South Africa, in four Tests, aged 40, he took 49 wickets at an average of 10.93. Next in the list of leading wicket-takers in a series is Jim Laker, with 46 for England in five Tests against Australia in 1956 (at an average of 9.60). Barnes never played for England again.

Barnes' career was highly unusual, especially for an English professional cricketer of his day, in that he played relatively little first-class cricket. He was born in Staffordshire, which has never been a first-class county. He played a handful of matches for Warwickshire between 1894 and 1896. He joined Lancashire in 1899 and played two full seasons in 1902 and 1903. Throughout his first-class career he played in no more than 133 first-class matches (he took five or more wickets in an innings 68 times in those matches, including Tests.)

Generally, the grind of county cricket did not appeal to Barnes. There was nothing sentimental about Barnes' approach to cricket. He played for money and he found that League and minor county cricket offered him a better deal. He remained an England regular for twelve years after he had effectively stopped playing county cricket. He played almost all his professional cricket for Staffordshire in the Minor Counties championship and for various leagues in Staffordshire and elsewhere. His record at this level was extraordinary. For Staffordshire, in 22 seasons, he took 1432 wickets at an average of eight.

He became a Test cricketer almost by accident, emerging from minor cricket obscurity after bowling to the Lancashire and England captain A. C. Maclaren in the nets at Old Trafford. Maclaren picked him for his side to tour Australia in 1901–02. In the first Test, in Sydney, England batted first and made 464 (Maclaren 116.) Australia had one and three quarter hours to bat on the second day. Barnes opened the bowling and soon had his first Test wicket, Trumper, caught and bowled for two. He bowled for the rest of the day, and then unchanged until just before lunch on the third day, when Australia's score was 132 for eight. He came back straight after lunch to take the last two wickets, finishing with five for 65 in 35.1 overs. England won by an innings and 124 runs (Barnes took one for 74 in the second innings.)

Australia fought back to win the second Test in Melbourne by 229 runs, but Barnes took 13 wickets in the match. Rain made for a spiteful wicket on the first day and Maclaren put the Australians in. Barnes (six for 42) and slow left-armer Colin Blythe bowled unchanged as Australia were dismissed for 112. England fared even worse, being bowled out for 61 (Gilbert Jessop 27.) The wicket improved on the second day. The Australian captain, Joe Darling reversed the batting order. Hill, batting at number seven, scored 99 and Warwick Armstrong and Reg Duff (104), each making his Test debut, put on 120 for the last wicket. Barnes bowled unchanged for 42 overs, taking six for 76, but suffered at the end like all the bowlers. He finished with seven for 121 off 64 overs, astonishing figures for a bowler in his second Test. Then Hugh Trumble and Monty Noble bowled England out for 175.

In the third test at Adelaide, Barnes was forced off the field with a twisted knee after bowling seven overs, and took no further part in the series, which Australia won four-one. The trip had been a valuable one for Barnes, not least because of the opportunity it gave him to observe the bowling of Noble. Noble, basically an off-spinner but with a mastery of swerve, "captivated Barnes," according to Fingleton, and he learned many variations from him. Noble himself singled Barnes out as the world's finest bowler.

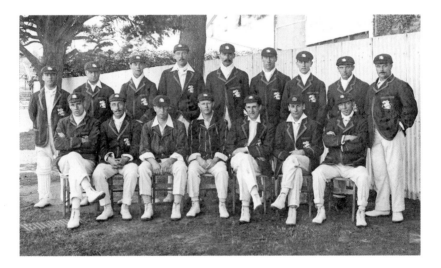

The MCC side that toured Australia in 1911-12. Sydney Barnes is seated far left in the front row, next to Wilfred Rhodes. Jack Hobbs is seated second from the right.

Strangely, though, he played only one game in the epic Ashes series of 1902, the third Test at Sheffield (the only Test played at that venue). Australia won by 143 runs to take a one-nil lead, but Barnes took six for 49 in 20 overs in the first innings, dismissing four of the top five including Duff, Darling and Hill. In his first spell he took three for seven in seven overs. Cardus was not alone in wondering what might have happened had he played in the pivotal fourth Test, at Old Trafford, which Australia won by three runs.

He next played for England in the Ashes series of 1907–08, which Australia won four-one. Barnes took 24 wickets at 26 apiece, including seven for 60 in Australia's first innings in the final Test in Sydney, but his most influential contribution to the series came, unpredictably, with the bat. England won the second Test, in Melbourne, by one wicket, and Barnes made a crucial 38 not out. In the 1909 Ashes series, which Australia won two-one, he played in the last three Tests, taking 17 wickets at 20 apiece.

His next international appearance, in the Ashes series of 1911–12, already referred to more than once, was to be the scene of perhaps his most memorable performance. Readers who have traversed this far will recall that this series was also the setting for substantial achievements by Jack Hobbs and Wilfred Rhodes. It was arguably England's greatest series win in Australia.

Australia won the first Test at Sydney by 146 runs. On the first morning of the next Test, at Sydney, conditions were very humid. The captains tossed and Hill won. "Bad luck, Johnny," he said to his opposite number, J. W. H. T. Douglas, "we'll bat."

At lunch, with some interruption for rain, Australia were 32 for four. Barnes had taken four for three in nine overs.

Charlie Kelleway played the first over from Foster very cautiously. Then Barnes prepared to bowl his first over to the left-hander Warren Bardsley, taking an age to set his field with Douglas; he was, "very pernickety," about such things, according to Fingleton. He then bowled Bardsley first ball. Hill came in next and scored a single off his first ball, the last run to be scored off Barnes for a while. Kelleway was out leg before in Barnes' third over. Then Hill was out to one that pitched on leg and hit the top of off stump: eight for three. Armstrong nicked his first ball from Barnes and was caught behind: eight for four.

Soon after this, as Trumper, batting later in the order than usual, and Vernon Ransford, were trying to restore some order, Barnes left the field feeling unwell.

After lunch Foster bowled Armstrong (33 for five) and then Barnes returned. Fred Minnett, having been dropped at third slip off Barnes, skied him to cover, where Hobbs took the catch: 38 for six. Barnes had taken five for six in eleven overs.

Fingleton, writing in 1956, called it, "Perhaps the most historic morning in Test history." England won the match by eight wickets. In the series as a whole Barnes took 34 wickets at 22.88, including two other five-wicket hauls. Remarkably, Barnes took 77 of his Ashes wickets in Australia.

In 1912 England hosted the Triangular Tournament involving Australia and South Africa, each side playing the others three times. England won four of their games, beating South Africa three times and Australia once. Australia won two of their games (both against South Africa) and South Africa none of theirs. Barnes had a phenomenal summer, taking 39 wickets at an average of 10.35 in England's first game against South Africa, Foster (five for 16) and Barnes (five for 25) bowled the visitors out for 58 in their first innings, and Barnes took six for 85 in the second. England won by an innings, Mr R. H. Spooner (as amateurs were designated in the *Wisden* scorecards of those days), making a century. The carnage continued in the later games against South Africa.

Barnes' mastery over the South Africans was confirmed on Douglas' MCC tour of 1913–14, when England won four of the five Tests. Barnes played in the first four games of which England won three, taking 49 wickets at an average of 10.93. This was on matting, which English bowlers were not used to. But, according to Cardus, Barnes on the mat was, "Probably as unplayable as mortal bowler has ever been." In the second Test, in Johannesburg, he took eight for 56 and nine for 103. Seventeen wickets in the match; this has been bettered once, by Laker who took nineteen Australian wickets at Old Trafford in 1956.

The fourth Test, in Durban, a draw in which Barnes took seven for 56 and seven for 88, was the last match he played for England. This can be partly accounted for by the outbreak of the First World War – Barnes was 46 when cricket resumed in 1919 – but not entirely.

He missed the fifth Test of the South African series, in Port Elizabeth, not because of ill health, as was reported at the time, but because he had a row with management about accommodation and expenses. One hears about modern administrators complaining of the problems of dealing with players like Kevin Pietersen and wonders what they might have made of Barnes.

He was actually selected for the Ashes tour of 1920–21. He asked for permission for his wife to join him on tour; permission was refused. When he learned that the captain, Douglas, was taking his entire family, including his parents, he declined the tour invitation. This also helps explain why he missed so many Tests in his heyday. "Plum" Warner refused to take him on the 1903–04 Ashes tour because of his "moods." He wasn't picked for the 1905 series either.

There was an incident in the first Test of the 1911–12 series, which England lost. Douglas won the toss and opted to field, taking the new ball himself, with Foster.

"What's he doing?" asked Barnes.

"He's goin' on first, Barney," answered Rhodes.

Barnes "glared," according to Cardus. It didn't happen again. Peter Gibbs – see below – said Barnes told him that Douglas, a boxing blue, was "…spoiling for a fight."

Portraits of the hatchet-faced Barnes – such as the celebrated one by Harry Rutherford hanging in the Pavilion at Lord's – make his aloof, austere character stand out. Even Cardus, clearly an admirer, had to admit that, "[t]here was something Mephistophelian about him." His humour, according to Cardus, was "pungent and cynical." He was nobody's fool and his pragmatic, money-centred attitude to the game must have made it difficult to deal with him. He remained a formidable cricketer long after he stopped playing for England; the West Indians who toured England in 1928 said he was the best bowler they faced. He kept working almost to the end (he lived to be 94), producing legal documents for Staffordshire County Council in his immaculate copperplate handwriting.

There is a wonderful essay in the 2012 *Wisden* by the author Peter Gibbs. He had been an obdurate opening batsman for Derbyshire in the late 1960s and was a particular *bete noire* of the brilliant *Times* journalist, Alan Gibson. When he heard that Gibbs was retiring, Gibson wrote that, "Derbyshire without P. J. K. Gibbs will be like *Hamlet* without the Second Gravedigger."

Anyway, Gibbs, an Oxford blue, learned his craft as a cricketer, like many distinguished professionals (notably the Derbyshire and England wicketkeeper Bob Taylor, and the "bank clerk who went to war," David Steele) in Staffordshire.

Barnes in an England touring blazer, 1903.

In his little masterpiece of an essay, Gibbs writes about the first day of a Minor Counties match between Staffordshire and Bedfordshire in 1964, which Barnes came to watch. Staffordshire's captain, the former England batsman Jack Ikin, delegated to Gibbs, as the youngest player in the side, the task of looking after Barnes (then aged 91). The role was not an easy one; the essay is entitled, *A Chill Wind Beyond the Boundary*. Ikin introduced Gibbs to Barnes as an Oxford blue. "The old boy looked as if he had been asked to accommodate a scorpion in his pants." The subject of Laker came up (he had been a pro with the club Gibbs played for). "Those pitches in '56 were a travesty. Money for old rope. What did he do in Australia?...Nobody got all 10 when I was bowling at the other end."

Bedfordshire batted first and were all out just before tea. Gibbs opened for Staffordshire and was out almost at once for nought. His stay in the middle was so brief that he hoped Barnes might have missed it, but he was sitting on the bench watching as Gibbs walked back.

Gibbs asked him to sign some scorecards for younger members. Barnes asked for a pen.

"A biro? Never touch them. An Oxford man should have a fountain pen."

Nothing was said about Gibbs' innings.

The day got worse. Derbyshire had to follow on, and Gibbs had to bat out an awkward 20 minutes. He was out second ball for another nought.

"The gloaming had descended prematurely and, though the lights of the clubroom glowed brightly, *SF* remained a shadowy figure under the lee of the pavilion veranda. My cheeks burned with rage and humiliation... I kept my head down until I reached the pavilion steps. Only then did I *steel* myself to look at him, but his eyes were fixed ahead, fingers wound round an imaginary ball, his mind still scheming to destroy better batsmen than me."

Barnes in a bowling pose, 1910.

Sydney Barnes

TESTS

Batting & Fielding

M	I	NO	Runs	HS	Ave	100	50	Ct
27	39	9	242	38*	8.06	0	0	12

Bowling

Balls	R	W	Ave	BBI	5	10	SR	Econ
7873	3106	189	16.43	9-103	24	7	41.65	

FIRST-CLASS

Batting & Fielding

M	I	NO	Runs	HS	Ave	100	50	Ct
133	173	50	1573	93	12.78	0.00	2	72

Bowling

Balls	R	W	Ave	BBI	5	10	Rate	
31521	12289	719.00	17.09	9-103	68	18	43.84	

Anderson acknowledges his five wicket haul against Australia at Edgbaston in 2009.

12

JAMES ANDERSON

Birth date	30 July 1982
Place of birth	Burnley, Lancashire
Role	Right-arm fast-medium bowler

The older James Anderson gets, the better he performs.

Obviously young fast bowlers start raw and improve as they get stronger and more mature. But that is not what we are talking about here. Anderson went through that phase years ago. He is now in the autumn of his career and he ought to be "slowing down". He is indeed slowing down. But in terms of pure skill, there is no diminution of his powers – quite the reverse.

In 2018 England played a five-Test home series against India and won it four-one, which was probably not a fair reflection of the two sides' respective merits.

The most interesting game of the series was the first Test, at Edgbaston (England's 1000th) which the hosts won by 31 runs.

The most intriguing passage of play in the match, perhaps in the summer, was the first innings duel between Anderson and the Indian captain Virat Kohli, the best batsman in the world – some were saying even better than the great Sachin Tendulkar (whom, incidentally, Anderson dismissed nine times in Tests, more than any other bowler).

Appetites had been whetted for this encounter, at least in England, by Kohli's record on India's previous visit, in 2014. England won that five-match series three-one, Anderson taking 25 wickets at an average of 20.60. In ten Test innings Kohli made 154 runs with a top score of 39. Anderson dismissed him four times; at Manchester he got him for nought (one of six ducks in India's first innings) and seven.

It was different in 2018, notwithstanding the series result. Kohli made 593 runs in the series, over 200 more than any other batsman on either side. And that day at Edgbaston saw two master craftsmen at work.

Anderson would, unexpectedly, star with the bat in Cardiff in 2009.

England had batted first and made 267. India's openers got off to a lively start but Sam Curran took two wickets and Kohli came in with the score on 54 for two, and it was soon 59 for three. Kohli started to rebuild. Anderson had a short and unsuccessful first spell but was soon back for a second. He bowled 15 consecutive overs, interrupted by lunch. For much of the time Kohli was facing him. At one stage Kohli scored off two balls out of 37 that Anderson bowled to him. Kohli played and missed, he edged, he groped forward and he huddled back. He looked decidedly uncomfortable. But he didn't get out. Then, off the last ball of the 15th over of that spell, he edged an outswinger to Dawid Malan at second slip – who dropped it. Kohli was on 21. There are no second chances with Kohli. He went on to make 149, and 51 in the second. (Hardik Pandya made 31 in the second innings; no other Indian batsman reached 30 in either innings.)

Anderson took four wickets for 91 runs in 38 overs at Edgbaston. But he did not dismiss Kohli once in the series.

In the series as a whole, Anderson, who turned 36 before the first Test, took 24 wickets at an average of 18.12. In the annihilation of India in the second Test at Lord's, when England won by an innings and 159 runs in less than three days' play – India's two innings took up a total of 82.3 overs – he took five for 20 and four for 23 in a total of 25.2 overs. In the course of this game he accomplished two significant landmarks. He took his hundredth Test wicket at Lord's; he finished with 103, more than anyone else at the great old ground. And, of more relevance to the point being made here – his career Test average fell below 27 for the first time since his debut year, 2003. (It had got as high as 39 in December 2007, a reflection of the difficulties he encountered after he initially burst on the international scene in 2003.) By the end of the series, he had added three further milestones to his record. First, he had taken more wickets in Tests against India (110) than anyone else. This is a testament to his longevity and also to the slightly cynical manoeuvring of the so-called Big Three (India, England and Australia) to ensure they play each other regularly: Anderson has played 27 Tests against India, more than any of the other leading wicket-takers; he has played only ten of those Tests in India, where he has taken 26 wickets. Secondly, he had bowled more balls in Tests than any other pace bowler. And, thirdly, with the last ball of the final Test, at The Oval, he overtook Glenn McGrath to become, with 564 wickets, the leading fast bowler in Tests.

England celebrate dismissing Australia for 98 in the 2010 Boxing Day Test.

In 2017, when he was a mere stripling of 35, he was statistically even more successful, albeit against arguably weaker opposition. In four Tests against South Africa (England won 3-1) he took 20 wickets at 14.10. In three Tests against West Indies (England won 2-1) he took 19 wickets, also at 14.10. In the West Indies' extraordinary win at Headingley he took five for 76 in their first innings, and in their second innings at Lord's he picked up seven for 42, his best figures in Tests. In the course of the match he took his 500th Test wicket.

"Bowling like this," said Hugh Chevallier, in his *Wisden* report, "... precise length, seductive swing, exquisite control – he looked good for 600 or more."

These achievements in 2017 and 2018 speak both of Anderson's longevity as a fast bowler and of his remarkable skill. The fact – noteworthy in its own way – that he failed to dismiss Kohli once in the 2018 series is not an indication of the waning of his powers; rather, it indicates the lengths, in terms of technical adjustment and concentration, that the world's best batsman was prepared to go to to ensure that he did not succumb to the world's best bowler.

In fact, the steady improvement in Anderson's record – the march to greatness – can be traced back further than 2017. From and including the calendar year 2014, he has played in 58 Tests and taken 235 wickets at an average of 21.62. These are remarkable figures in what has often been regarded as a batsman-friendly era (although openers have struggled, especially in England). Anderson himself wrote, in 2019, "In the last five or six years everything has fallen into place. My action and skills are as good as they have ever been and I feel really confident bowling in all conditions."

During that period, apart from the instances already mentioned, there were some striking match-winning performances. The second Test against West Indies at Grenada in 2014–15 seemed to be heading for the series' second attritional draw as the final day began with six West Indian second innings wickets still standing. Anderson won the game almost single-handed. He dismissed three leading batsmen – centurion Kraigg Brathwaite, caught at slip off a rearing delivery, Shiv

Chanderpaul, edging to Alastair Cook at slip, and Marlon Samuels caught behind – for one run in 23 balls. He then held two catches and took the last wicket by running out Jason Holder by a direct hit from mid-off. England won by eight wickets. In the first Test against Sri Lanka at Headingley in 2016, he took five for 16 in 11.4 overs and five for 29 in 13.3 overs as England won by an innings and 88 runs.

"One of his insouciantly brilliant spells," said Jonathan Liew, "the sort that renders the middle of the bat superfluous."

It was growing consistency as well as immense skill that led Cook, his then captain, to state at the end of the India series in 2014: "He is the greatest bowler England has ever produced." It seemed a bit extravagant then. Now, somehow, it doesn't seem so far-fetched.

Anderson has been a principal beneficiary of two particular developments affecting English cricket. The first has been the central contracts system introduced under the watch of ECB chairman Lord (Ian) MacLaurin. This has enabled the England management to control the amount of cricket played by their key players. In that 2018 season Anderson played two Tests against Pakistan as well as five against India. For his county, Lancashire, he played three matches, bowling exactly 100 overs and taking nine wickets for 280 runs.

It's interesting to compare Anderson's workload in 2018 with Fred Trueman's in 1963. Trueman, then aged 32, took 34 wickets against a strong West Indian side at an average of 17.47. He also played 18 three-day matches for Yorkshire and other teams. Anderson has played 246 first-class matches in his career, which started in 2002, 149 of which have been Tests, so he has played only 97 "ordinary" first-class matches in 20 seasons. Trueman played 603 first-class matches, of which 67 were Tests. Of course there was one other big difference. Trueman's five Tests against West Indies were played between 6 June and 26 August (the tourists themselves played 30 first-class matches in all). Anderson's five Tests against India were played between 1 August and 11 September (India played one (non first-class) three-day match, against Essex, to many judges a key factor in their disappointing performance in the Tests.) Anyway, it is hard to believe that the ability to give Anderson a break from first-class cricket – and the fact that he stopped playing one-day internationals after the 2015 World Cup – have not helped prolong his Test career. Bowlers like Trueman and Alec Bedser believed the best way for a bowler to get fit was to bowl, as opposed to doing gym work. As it happens, Anderson has been remarkably fit throughout his career. Until relatively recently it has been rare for him to miss a game through injury. In fact Anderson's philosophy is not so different from Bedser's.

"There's nothing better for me, even if I don't get wickets, than bowling 25 overs in a day and when I'm walking off, everything is killing."

A second factor has been the use of the Dukes cricket ball in England (and West Indies). Everywhere else the Australian-made Kookaburra ball is used. The Dukes ball, with its tighter-stitched and more pronounced seam, has certainly helped Anderson, a master swing bowler. His record in Australia is perfectly respectable but nothing like as good as his record in England. In the 2017–18 Ashes, won by Australia four-nil, he took 17 wickets at an average of 27.82. This was considerably better than any other England bowler, but Australia's three pacemen, Pat Cummins, Josh Hazlewood and Mitchell Starc, were taller and faster, and each took more wickets at a cheaper cost. It is not just the ball of course – conditions generally are very different in places like Australia and India. But the Dukes ball is definitely Anderson's weapon of choice.

Although not everything went to plan, Anderson claimed five wickets during England's victory at the MCG in 2010. England won by an innings and 158 runs.

Anderson's average per wicket is higher (34) against Australia than against anyone else but that does not mean he hasn't enjoyed significant success against them. After all, in his career as an England player, which started in 2003, England have played nine Ashes series, of which they have won five and drawn one. He narrowly missed out on getting an OBE in 2005 – that honour, for replacing Simon Jones in The Oval Test – went to Paul Collingwood. His greatest achievement in an Ashes series came in Andrew Strauss' triumphant three-one series win in 2010–11, when England won three matches by an innings, a unique achievement in an Ashes series. Despite having to use Kookaburra balls, Anderson found sufficient swing to cause real problems to the Australian top order, as when he dismissed Ricky Ponting and Michael Clarke on the first morning at the Adelaide Oval to reduce Australia to two for three.

"To think that there had been so much learned debate before the series about Anderson's ability to swing the Kookaburra," wrote Gideon Haigh, "here he was making it laugh." And when it simply wouldn't swing, he found other ways to get batsmen out. Under the tutelage of England's bowling coach, the Australian David Saker, Anderson discovered the "wobble seam". For this delivery, the fingers were slightly wider either side of the seam and, instead of relying on strong wrist support behind the ball, the key to his swing bowling, the ball was "released" rather than pushed out. Ideally it would land on the edge of the seam. In Anderson's view, if he didn't know which way it was going to move, the batsman certainly didn't. It was this series that saw him emerge as a "complete" bowler. He finished with 24 wickets (at 26.04), the best return of any English fast bowler in Australia since John Snow in 1970–71.

On the whole though he has thrived against Australia in English conditions. He was the key to home success in a tense first Test at Trent Bridge in 2013, taking five for 85 and, on a gripping final day, five for 73. He bowled superbly on that final day, confirming, said Haigh, "His transformation from a classically English swing bowler to the best paceman in the world in dry conditions… He is as classically English now as chicken tikka masala." In the third Test of the 2015 series, at Edgbaston, which England won by eight wickets, Australia were bundled out for 136 in their first innings, Anderson taking six for 47.

Edgbaston has always been a favourite ground for England but for Anderson Trent Bridge has often brought success. This can rarely have been seen to better effect than in the first Test against Pakistan in 2010, when he took five for 54 in 22 overs and six for 17 in 15 overs (Pakistan were all out for 80) in the second, on his 28th birthday. According to Ramiz Raja's *Wisden* match report "Anderson's side-on arched body with bolt-upright wrist made a perfect set-up for swing bowling."

Another factor which has been a help to Anderson has been having the same opening bowling partner for so long. He and Stuart Broad first opened together in 2009 and, with occasional forced separations because of injury, have been together ever since. They complement each other perfectly. Broad is taller, hits the deck harder, extracts more bounce and relies more on seam movement than on swing. He also has the remarkable capacity, all of a sudden, to produce an unplayable spell. They are the most successful opening bowling partnership ever, in terms of wickets taken together. Anderson is obviously the senior partner. The feeling seems to be growing, not surprisingly given Anderson's age, that the end of the alliance is nigh. Broad seems to rise to the occasion when Anderson is missing. After his six for 47 at Edgbaston in 2015 everyone thought that Anderson would be rubbing his hands with glee at the prospect of the next Test, at Trent Bridge, but he had strained his side at Edgbaston and missed the final two games. Broad took eight for 15 at Trent Bridge. In the 2019 Ashes, where Anderson's contribution was limited to four overs in the first Test because of a calf injury, Broad had his most productive series for years.

Both of them seemed surplus to requirements in the series against Sri Lanka in 2017–18 when they played three Tests and took one wicket between them. But Anderson's impact on the series was not negligible. In the second Test at Pallekele, which England won by 57 runs, he was involved in last wicket stands of 60 and 41 (he made seven and 12).

This of course was far from the first time that the "Burnley Lara" had shone with the bat. Early in his Test career he earned a curious reputation for never getting out for nought; he made one duck in his first 60 Test innings (he has made up for this since). His first significant contribution in an Ashes Test came in the first Test of the 2009 series at Cardiff. This was a game Australia appeared to be in complete control of to the very end. They responded to England's 415 with 674 for six (four batsmen made centuries). Rain caused the loss of a session on the fourth day and England began the fifth with two wickets down and still 219 adrift. Wickets fell steadily. Collingwood was the real hero; he made 74 in nearly six hours. With his departure, last man Monty Panesar joined Anderson in the middle. There were 11.3 overs to go. Amazingly they survived. As Anderson has written, "We had been absolutely beaten into the ground for pretty much five whole days and yet it was cause for celebration." Strauss' team went on to regain the Ashes.

In the first Test against India at Trent Bridge in 2014, a rather dreadful draw, he made 81, and put on 198 for the tenth wicket with Joe Root, a world record. One suspects Anderson spends more time thinking about another 10th-wicket stand. Just three weeks earlier, in the second Test against Sri Lanka at Headingley, England went into the fifth day in an apparently hopeless position – 57 for five chasing a notional 350. Even a draw seemed impossible; no side had saved a game going into the last day with five down. But Moeen Ali played the – defensive – innings of his life, scoring 108 not out off 281 balls, a maiden century in his second Test. Last man Anderson kept him company for 81 minutes as England crept towards safety. With just two balls to go Anderson popped a sharply lifting ball into the hands of forward short leg; the match, and the series, had been lost.

It would be an exaggeration to say that Anderson went straight from Burnley Thirds to England but it did almost seem like that. In fact Anderson himself has always acknowledged the debt he owes to Mike Watkinson, Lancashire's bowling coach for helping fine tune his action, periodically the object of unwelcome attention from coaches in the England set-up. The perceived problem with his action was a curious dip of his head as he delivered the ball. This was felt by the coaches to be potentially dangerous; in fact the real issue was that it wasn't quite "normal". Hence, attempts were made to change it.

After making his Lancashire debut in 2002 he went to Australia with the Academy team that winter and made his England debut in a one-day international against Australia at the Adelaide Oval, taking one for 12 in 10 overs.

2003 was an exciting year, including an impressive World Cup in South Africa, marred only by a final over in the exciting game against Australia which saw Andy Bichel whack England out of the tournament. He took a five for one Test debut against Zimbabwe at Lord's. He was becoming a star. He was a fast bowler, which helps. He looked good, which is even better. A little later he became the first cricketer to be the subject of a nude photograph. People thought – at least hoped – he

might be cricket's answer to David Beckham. But then things started
to go wrong. He was much faster then than he is now and he hadn't
worked out his own strengths; a lot of energy was expended on bowling
bouncers. This was also the period when his action was being tweaked
at the suggestion of the England coaching staff. There were injury
problems, including, ironically, a stress fracture of the back in 2006, and
he was in and out of the team.

*Anderson celebrates the fall of an Australian wicket at the Adelaide Oval in
2010.*

It was only really on the tour of New Zealand in 2007–08, under
the management of Peter Moores, that he started being given more
responsibility, choosing the ball, and gradually assuming a leadership
role as the old guard, Matthew Hoggard and Steve Harmison, moved
on. In 2008, at Trent Bridge – where else? – he took seven for 43 against

New Zealand. And something seemed to click. By this time his bowling action had been restored to its original form, surely a significant fact.

He seems a different person now. The rather bolshy fast bowler is an engaging and humorous character, a cult figure in the popular radio show/podcast Tailenders. In the cricket world, he is Jimmy. To family and close non-cricketing friends he has always been James. Explaining the ubiquitous use of Jimmy to his mother is something to which he has become accustomed. Writing about the naming of the James Anderson End, at Old Trafford (itself, a "surreal experience"), he observed "At least she got that one."

His bowling, as was said at the start, gets better and better. His stock ball is the outswinger. He has a smooth, easy and not too long run-up and the perfect outswinger's action, with his curious quirk, mentioned earlier, of appearing to look at the ground by his foot as he delivers. He can mix it with inswingers, where his action barely changes, and when the conditions are right he will bowl cutters (off, mostly, but leg too). And he is still improving. In 2017 the South African opening bowler Vernon Philander (whose figures in England's first innings in the first Test at Centurion in December 2019 were 14.2 – 6 –16 – 4) toured England; he bowled at 78 mph and was, according to Anderson, "unplayable." In his book Anderson said that he learned a lot from watching him.

And then there is reverse swing. Pakistan may have invented it but England have long been proficient; Simon Jones gave a masterclass in the 2005 Ashes. "Ball management" is the key. Anderson has long played a critical role for England there. On that New Zealand tour he took over from Ryan Sidebottom the task of selecting the match balls. When Cook was captain the job of shining the ball was left exclusively to the captain and his premier fast bowler. Reverse swing played a key role at Melbourne in 2010–11. Tim Paine may have been only half joking when he said that "Sandpapergate" had put a stop to it. Anderson's view is that English weather makes it more unlikely that the combination of circumstances that are necessary for reverse swing to materialise will occur.

Anderson was the first English bowler to reach 400, 500 and 600 wickets in Test matches.

India is a different matter. The new ball will swing. Then it's up to the spinners. But the abrasive nature of the pitch, and the dry conditions, mean that reverse may play its part. Even the experts can't really explain reverse though. In 2012–13, Cook's first series in charge, Anderson helped England secure a rare series win taking 10 wickets in the last two games. The Indian captain M. S. Dhoni, said he was, "The difference between the sides." Anderson takes up the story.

At Nagpur "I bowled Sachin Tendulkar with one that reversed back in. The ground went really quiet. You could feel it in shock. It wasn't quiet in my head. I couldn't believe it had happened."

In 2018 he was the complete master. As George Dobell observes, "He is not perfect: he and Broad can be irritatingly wasteful of the new ball. But he is a joy to watch." It is perhaps no longer sensible to refer to him as a fast bowler. He now bowls at around 80 mph. But he is so much more dangerous than he was as a youngster. Like McGrath and Philander, he approaches the task of dismissing opposing batsmen with the patience of a saint and the finesse of a surgeon.

Root, his latest captain, said he was, "…at his best," in 2018. That may well have been true. When he knocked Mohammed Shami's middle stump out of the ground on that final day of The Oval Test to beat McGrath's record people were talking about his eclipsing Anil Kumble's 619 Test wickets. Maybe he will. He is 43 behind at the time of writing (after the first Boxing Day Test against South Africa in 2019–20.)

That Oval Test was Cook's last, memorably marked by his scoring a century, as he had done in his first also against India, in Nagpur, in 2005–06. Anderson, like Cook, was flown in as a replacement on that tour, though he did not play in Nagpur. Anderson was visibly affected by Cook's retirement. That is hardly surprising. They had been through so much together. There were the triumphs – The Ashes in 2010–11 and 2013, India in 2012 /13. There were the disasters, including two Ashes whitewashes. It was a remarkable and happy coincidence that they were respectively England's greatest Test run-scorer and wicket-taker. Cook was only 33 when he retired.

2019 was a difficult year for Anderson, the calf injury sustained in the first Ashes Test keeping him out of the rest of the series and the next one in New Zealand. Every England supporter will be hoping he is back to his best, and by the time this book is published, we will know. Whatever happens, Anderson has played a memorable role in England's cricket history.

James Anderson

TESTS

Batting & Fielding

M	I	NO	Runs	HS	Ave	100	50	Ct
149	209	87	1181	81	9.68	0	1	91

Bowling

Balls	R	W	Ave	BBI	5	10	SR	Econ
32359	15491	575	26.94	7–42	27	3	56.2	2.87

ONE-DAY INTERNATIONALS

Batting & Fielding

M	I	NO	Runs	HS	Ave	SR	100	50	Ct
194	79	43	273	28	7.58	48.66	0	0	53

Bowling

Balls	R	W	Ave	BBI	5	SR	Econ
9584	7861	269	29.22	5–23	2	35.60	4.92

FIRST-CLASS

Batting & Fielding

M	I	NO	Runs	HS	Ave	100	50	Ct
246	316	127	1822	81	9.64	0	1	144

Bowling

Balls	R	W	Ave	BBI	5	10	SR	Econ
49485	23728	950	24.97	7–42	47	6	52	2.87

Portrait of Sydney Barnes, by H. Rutherford, hanging in the Pavilion at Lord's. Peter Gibbs described it as "a portrait of intimidation".

13

AFTERWORD

COVID19

Naturally there was a contractual deadline for producing this book: I had to deliver it to the publishers by the end of December 2019.

I managed to do that. A launch was tentatively scheduled for June 2020, coinciding with the Lord's Test against West Indies.

Ah well, we all know what happened then. But the summer was not lost. The England and Wales Cricket Board did a magnificent job in hosting two three-match Test series, against West Indies and Pakistan, in bio-secure bubbles in Manchester and Southampton. The cricketing world owes a huge debt of gratitude to the players and administrators of the visiting teams for agreeing to tour England in those extraordinary circumstances.

And, of course, two of 'my' players took part in both series and they both continued to show why they have to be selected in an eleven such as this. Ben Stokes continued his astonishing run of form, making a magnificent 176 in the second Test against West Indies and taking vital wickets when his team needed a breakthrough. He dropped a few catches, and England lost his first Test as captain. Meanwhile, the indestructible James Anderson, on a soggy August day in Southampton, became the first pace bowler to take 600 hundred Test wickets.

Oh, and Sir Ian Botham was ennobled, for services to Brexit.

Let's hope that by the time this book is published, life, and cricket, are back to normal.

Bill Ricquier

September 2020, Singapore

Wilfred Rhodes' first class career lasted for over 30 years. This shot was taken in 1906.

14

ACKNOWLEDGEMENTS

I have a lot of people to thank. First on the list, chronologically, must be the literary agent Susan Mears, because it was she who introduced me to Lisa Hanrahan and the team at Rockpool Publishing. So it can truly be said that, without Susan, although this book would have existed, it would not have been written by me.

I know the book would have existed because it is part of a series and I have realised that when Lisa wants something done, it gets done. She has been fantastic to work with, as have Luke West and the whole team at Rockpool/Gelding Street Press. It says something that they maintained faith in the project through the pandemic.

Lisa introduced me to an editor, Christopher Cyrill. Christopher has been a revelation to work with. I have written several books (including a land law text book in its fifth edition) but I have never worked with such an interested and exacting editor. Lots of changes were made thanks to his sage advice. On those rare occasions – they did happen – when he said, "Excellent chapter; great use of detail", it really meant something.

My friends Derek and Chantal Hudson have been astonishingly generous with their time and effort, whether it be technological assistance (Lisa and the team would have been alarmed to know how technologically ill-equipped I am, though I suspect Christopher must have guessed), proof reading first drafts, and Derek's help with the choice of images. Contractual and regulatory issues meant we could not use all the images originally selected, but Luke and the team sourced some terrific pictures. The look of the book is so important.

Jean-Noel Coster was also incredibly helpful on the technological side. And now we have a Frenchman who knows something about S.F. Barnes.

I also need to thank Vic Marks for providing a perfect cover quote, my indispensable secretary Wati Kassim, Jemima and Dicky Barton, Malcolm Merry, William Shaw, David Edwards, Steve Eason, Chelva Rajah, Jacques and Cornelia Merkt, Piers Pottinger, Kristy Hewitt, Gordon Wignall, Henrietta Cottam, Tom Inglis and Kim Seah.

Anita and Guy have of course been steadfast in their support. We moved out of and back into our home in the course of this book being written, a project brilliantly masterminded by Anita and managed by Queenie. The cricket library has not just survived, but prospered.

Bill Ricquier

15

BIBLIOGRAPHY

Anderson, James and White, Felix. *Bowl, Sleep, Repeat.* Cassell, London, 2019

Arlott, John. *Fred.* Eyre & Spottiswoode, London, 1971.

Arlott, John. *Jack Hobbs: A Profile of The Master.* John Murray Publishers, London, 1981.

Arlott, John. *Vintage Summer.* Eyre & Spottiswoode, London, 1967.

Barker, Ralph and Rosenwater, Irving. *Test Cricket: England v Australia.* B. T. Batsford Ltd, London, 1969.

Benaud, Richie. *A Tale of Two Tests.* Hodder and Stoughton, London, 2015.

Berry, Scyld. Cricket The *Game of Life.* Hodder & Stoughton, London, 2015.

Botham, Ian. *My Autobiography.* Collins Willow, London, 1994.

Brearley, Mike. *Phoenix From The Ashes.* Hodder & Stoughton, London, 1982

–, *On Cricket,* Constable, London, 2018.

Cardus, Neville, *A Fourth Innings With Cardus.* Souvenir Press, London, 1987.

–, *Australian Summer,* Souvenir Press, London, 1957, reprinted Jonathan Cape Ltd, 1987.

–, *Close of Play,* Collins. London, 1956.

–, *Play Resumed With Cardus.* (Reprint of extracts from earlier published books), Souvenir Press, London, 1979.

–, *The Playfair Cardus,* The Dickens Press, London, 1963.

Chalke, Stephen. *At The Heart of English Cricket.* Fairfield Books, Bath, 2001.

Fingleton, Jack. *Brightly Fades The Don.* Collins, London, 1949.

–, *Cricket Crisis.* Cassell and Company Ltd, Melbourne, 1946.

–, *Fingleton on Cricket.* Collins, London, 1973.

–, *The Ashes Crown The Year.* Collins, London, 1954.

Foot, David. *Wally Hammond: The Reasons Why.* Robson Books, London, 1996.

Frindall, Bill. *England Test Cricketers.* William Collins & Co Ltd, London, 1989.

Gower, David, *David Gower's 50 Greatest Cricketers Of All Time,* Icon Books Limited, 2015.

Haigh, Gideon. *The Summer Game.* Text Publishing, Melbourne 1997.

–, *Ashes 2011,* Aurum Press Ltd, London, 2011

–, *Ashes To Ashes,* Simon & Schuster, London, 2014.

Hamilton, Duncan. *The Great Romantic.* Hodder & Stoughton, London, 2019.

Heald, Tim. *Denis Compton.* P avilion Books, London, 1994.

Hutton, Len. *Just My Story.* The Sportsmans Book Club, London, 1957.

Kilburn, J. M. *Cricket Decade.* William Heinemann, London, 1959.

–, *Thanks To Cricket.* Sportsmans Book Club, Newton Abbot, 1973.

Marks, Vic, *Original Spin: Misadventures In Cricket.* Atlantic Books, London, 2019.

Martin-Jenkins, Christopher, *The Top 100 Cricketers Of All Time,* Corinthian Books, London, 2009.

Mason, Ronald. *Walter Hammond: A Biography.* Hollis & Carter Ltd, London, 1962.

McKinstry, Leo. *Jack Hobbs, England's Greatest Cricketer,* Yellow Jersey Press, London, 2011.

Nicholls, J. L. *The Legendary Cricket Genius Sydney F. Barnes*. Self-published, 2018.

Peebles, Ian. *Denis Compton*. Macmillan, London, 1971.

Plumptre, George, Swanton, E. W. and
    Woodcock, John (Eds). *Barclays World
    of Cricket, The Game From A-Z*. William Collins & Co, London, 1986.

Pringle, Derek. *Pushing The Boundaries*. Hodder & Stoughton, London, 2018.

Robinson, Ray. *Between Wickets*. Fontana Books, London, 1958.

Ross Alan, Ed. *The Cricketer's Companion*, Eyre & Spottiswoode, London, 1963.

–, *West Indies At Lord's*, Constable, London, 1996.

Trueman, Fred. *As it Was: The Memoirs of Fred Trueman*. Macmillan, London, 2004.

Wilde, Simon. *Number One*. Victor Gollancz, London, 1998.

–, *England: The Biography*. Simon & Schuster, London, 2018.

Woodcock, John. *The Times One Hundred Greatest Cricketers*. Macmillan, London 1998.

Websites:
The Cricketer.
https://www.thecricketer.com/

ESPNcricinfo.
https://www.espncricinfo.com/

Wisden Cricketers' Almanack.
Online archive: 1864-2015
https://www.wisden.com/

ABOUT THE
AUTHOR

Bill Ricquier was born and raised in Winchester, England. He has vivid memories of his first visit to the County Ground at Northlands Road, Southampton, to watch Hampshire play Kent; cricket has been a passion ever since. He is the author of two books on cricket, *The Indian Masters* , and *The Pakistani Masters*. Each was published in England and India. He is also a co-author of *Hampshire: 100 Greats*. He has published articles for a variety of publications, including Scoreline (for whom he covered the men's World Cup in 2019), and *ESPNcricinfo*. His blog, From The Pavilion End (@billpavilionend.com) has been covering cricket, historical and current, since 2014.

Bill lives with his wife and son in Singapore, where he has worked for many years practising and teaching law.

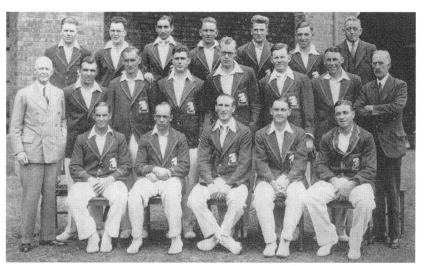

Wally Hammond, front right, was the equal top run-scorer during The Ashes series of 1932-33.

ACK HOBBS · LEN HUTTON · WAL
ALAN KNOTT · WILFRED RHODE
OBBS · LEN HUTTON · WALLY HA
LAN KNOTT · WILFRED RHODES
OBBS · LEN HUTTON · WALLY HA
LAN KNOTT · WILFRED RHODES
OBBS · LEN HUTTON · WALLY HA
LAN KNOTT · WILFRED RHODES
OBBS · LEN HUTTON · WALLY HA
LAN KNOTT · WILFRED RHODES
OBBS · LEN HUTTON · WALLY HA
LAN KNOTT · WILFRED RHODES
OBBS · LEN HUTTON · WALLY HA
LAN KNOTT · WILFRED RHODES
OBBS · LEN HUTTON · WALLY HA
LAN KNOTT · WILFRED RHODES
OBBS · LEN HUTTON · WALLY HA
LAN KNOTT · WILFRED RHODES
OBBS · LEN HUTTON · WALLY H